BOTH JOAN RIVIERE AND MELANIE KLEIN played significant roles in the development of the psychoanalytic movement in England and the English-speaking world. Joan Riviere is best known for her inspired translations of Freud's writings. As James Strachey has said, her translation of the *Introductory Lectures* in the 1920's "made it possible for the first time for readers of English to realize that Freud was not only a master of science but a master of prose writing." Mrs. Riviere studied with Freud in Vienna in 1922 and several years later began practicing as a lay analyst in London. In later life she devoted herself to painstaking editing and translating for the *International Journal of Psychoanalysis.*

Melanie Klein was a pioneer in the field of child psychoanalysis and was the first person to concentrate on the development of analytic techniques uniquely suited to children. Her book *The Psychoanalysis of Children* is a full report of her contribution to this important area of psychoanalysis. With Paula Heimann, Susan Isaacs, and Joan Riviere she is also the author of *Developments in Psychoanalysis.*

LOVE, HATE
AND REPARATION

MELANIE KLEIN

JOAN RIVIERE

W · W · NORTON & COMPANY

New York · London

FIRST PUBLISHED IN THE NORTON LIBRARY 1964

W. W. Norton & Company, Inc. is also the publisher of the works of Erik H. Erikson, Otto Fenichel, Karen Horney, Harry Stack Sullivan, and The Standard Edition of the Complete Psychological Works of Sigmund Freud.

ISBN 0-393-00260-8

W. W. Norton & Company, Inc., 500 Fifth Avenue, New York, NY 10110
W. W. Norton & Company Ltd, 10 Coptic Street, London WC1A 1PU

PRINTED IN THE UNITED STATES OF AMERICA

PREFACE

THIS book is something of a new departure in psycho-analytical exposition. An attempt is made to convey in everyday language some of the deeper mental processes which underlie the everyday actions and feelings of normal men and women. The subject has not been treated in this way before, and it requires the reader to adjust his thought in order to appreciate the way the mind works in the unconscious. The evidence for the conclusions is not given here, the book would have to be at least twenty times as large if it were. The long and painful struggle which the individual goes through during his attempt to deal with these unconscious processes in himself, the way in which he tries to push intolerable thoughts and impulses out of his consciousness, and finally, his growing awareness that when these buried thoughts are brought to light they do explain things about himself which are otherwise inexplicable—all this material, which is available to the analyst and which alone is convincing, has had to be left out.

The reader should be on his guard against two tendencies which, if given play, would lead to a misconstruction of the theme that is to follow. He should try to avoid the mistake of attributing to the conscious minds of young children such mental processes as only develop later. Also he must remember that the unconscious has laws of mental functioning quite other than those of the more reason-loving and conscious levels of the mind. Not a little misunderstanding of psycho-analysis is due to a

failure to grasp the fact that unconscious ways of
thought and feeling are not only unconscious but are
grasped only with difficulty.

In this exposition the authors have traced many
things in the adult back to their origins in infancy
and have shown many features in the adult which
are evidence of the persistence of early modes of
thinking. This switching back and forth from child
to adult, and adult to child, is inherent in the topic
and may at first seem puzzling. The fact is that the
unconscious of the adult is actually not so very
different from the mind of the child ; it must be
recognized, therefore, that in a certain sense psycho-
analysts do attribute infantile thinking to grown-
ups, while at the same time distinguishing between
the adult and the infantile personality and mode of
thought. The work on which this book is based
largely derives from Mrs. Klein's researches into
the early development of the emotional and mental
life of the child. It is proper to say that these researches and the conclusions drawn from them are
still undergoing the tests of criticism and further
application.

The series, of which this book is the second number,
is not confined to abridgements and reprints of
' psycho-analytical classics ' ; it includes recent
work when, as in this book, the views put forward
show a capacity for constructive expansion and
development, and illuminate problems that were
formerly obscure.

JOHN RICKMAN.

11 Kent Terrace,
    Regent's Park,
        London, N.W.1.
July 1937.

CONTENTS

(The two parts of this book are based on public lectures delivered under the auspices of the Institute of Psycho-Analysis in March 1936, at the Caxton Hall, Westminster, under the general title of ' The Emotional Life of Civilized Men and Women.')

HATE, GREED AND AGGRESSION

By Joan Riviere

HATE, GREED AND AGGRESSION

In this book we discuss some aspects of the emotional
life of ordinary men and women in civilized com-
munities, the everyday manifestations of which are
familiar to all of us. Two of the ultimate sources
of these familiar emotional manifestations are the
two great primary instincts of man : hunger and
love, or the self-preservative and the sexual instincts. Essentially our lives are devoted to a double
aim, to securing the means of our existence and to
getting pleasure out of it as well. We all know that
these aims give rise to deep emotions and can be
the occasion of great happiness or unhappiness.
Now, to present a picture of the interaction of
self-preservation, pleasure, love and hate adequately
would be the same thing as to describe and explain
every manifestation of human life. Our efforts to
sketch a rough outline of it in these two lectures
must necessarily be simplified and schematic to a
high degree, and full of gaps. We are merely trying
to give you an idea of some of the main patterns of
emotional life, as they work out in the behaviour
of individuals or types. It should be borne in mind
that, broadly speaking, hate is a destructive dis-
integrating force, tending towards privation and
death, and love a harmonizing unifying one, tending to life and pleasure. But this needs immediate
qualification ; for aggression, which is closely
allied to hate, is by no means entirely destructive or painful, either in its aims or functioning ;
and love, which springs from the life-forces and

3

is so closely linked with desire, can be aggressive
and even destructive in its operation. The fundamental aim in life is to live and to live pleasurably.
In order to achieve this, each of us tries to deal with
and dispose of the destructive forces in himself,
venting, diverting and fusing them in such a way
as to obtain the maximum *security* he can in life—
and pleasures to boot—an aim which we achieve
by infinitely various, subtle and complicated adaptations. The different outcome in each individual
is in the main the product of two varying factors :
the strength of the love and hate tendencies (the
emotional forces in each of us) and the influence of
environment throughout life on each of us, these
two factors being in constant interaction from
birth till death. In this lecture I shall describe
some of the ways in which we endeavour to deal with
and obtain *security* against the dangerous disinte-
grating forces of hate and aggression in ourselves
which, if too strong, may lead to painful privations or
even to extinction.

Aggression

An instinct of aggression, at any rate for defence,
is generally recognized as innate in man and most
animals. It seems clear, too, that aggressive impulses are a radical and basic element in human
psychology ; we have only to look at the international situation, or at the behaviour in any
nursery, to see that. But quite apart from ' outside
evidence,' so to speak, I think every ordinary
person knows from his own experience that bad
temper, selfishness, meanness, greediness, jealousy
and enmity are being felt and expressed all round
him every day by others, even if he does not

appreciate their existence so well in himself. He certainly knows that a great part of the unhappiness of everyday life arises from such feelings. Most of us have to spend some proportion at least of our time and energies in trying to overcome and mitigate the bad effects of them when shown by others—and also indeed when manifested by ourselves.

We know too that aggressive, cruel and selfish impulses are closely bound up with pleasure and gratification, that there can be a fascination or an excitement accompanying gratification of these feelings. For instance, the savage satisfaction, or at least the glee, felt by someone making a cutting retort can often be seen in his eyes. Bloodcurdling and cruel stories, pictures, films, sports, accidents, atrocities, etc., are exciting in greater or lesser degree to all human beings who have not learnt to modify this tendency or to deflect it elsewhere. Most of us feel an elation which is pleasurable on overcoming an obstacle, or on getting our own way. This *pleasure* that is apt to be closely linked with aggressive emotions explains to some extent why they are so imperative, and difficult to control. It is also evident that aggression in certain forms plays a considerable part in the struggle for existence. In all fields of work, and in pleasures, too, we recognize clearly that people who have not enough aggression, who cannot assert themselves enough against obstacles, are deficient in a valuable quality. We can in fact say that both the self-preservative and ' love ' instincts need a certain admixture of aggression if they are to attain satisfaction, that is, an aggressive element is an essential part of both these instincts in actual functioning.

Now, though we all know, or ought to know, that aggressive feelings do exist in ourselves and in others, on the whole we do not much like the idea of them, so unconsciously we minimize and underestimate their importance. We do not focus our eyes on them, but keep them in the outer edges of our field of vision and do not let them form part of our whole picture of life ; by keeping them a little blurred, they do not appear so near and vivid, so real and vital, and thus so alarming as they would be if we saw them clearly. This of course is a very primitive method of dealing with our fear of them ; it is only comforting to ourselves and not really advantageous. One condition of scientific work, however, is that one cannot select some parts of a thing for close examination and leave others on one side ; consequently psycho-analysis has learnt that these well-known but unpleasant things are much more significant and wider in their bearings, more *dynamic*, than they are usually felt to be.

One explanation for hostile emotions is evident, at least in many cases, namely, that the people feeling them are discontented and dissatisfied with their lot or their conditions. Whether it is some necessary of life or some pleasure they cannot obtain, they have a sense of loss. It is self-evident that an attack, or attempt to rob or hurt and so cause him a loss, will rouse aggression in any ordinary person, and in most animals. But there is another source of the feeling of loss and pain besides that of an attack from without. An *unfulfilled desire* within us can, if intense enough, create a similar sense of loss and pain, and so rouse aggression in exactly the same way as an attack. This human reaction has a great bearing on economic questions ; it is well known that a lack of the means of subsistence in peoples and classes rouses their aggression, unless they are in a condition of hopeless apathy, despair and inertia.[1] Another point, which economists realize much better perhaps than other people do, is the degree of *dependence* of the human organism on its surroundings. In a stable political and economic system there is a great deal of apparent liberty and opportunity to fulfil our own needs, and we do not as a rule feel our dependence on the organization in which we live—unless, for instance, there is an earthquake or a strike! Then we may realize with reluctance and often with deep resentment that we are dependent on the forces of nature or on other people to a terrifying extent. Dependence is felt to be dangerous because it involves the possibility of privation. An unrealizable desire for individual self-sufficiency may arise, and an illusion of an independent liberty may under certain conditions of life be indulged in as a pleasure in itself.

There is one great exception to this, however—one situation in life where we all must feel dependent, whatever our circumstances—and that is in love-relations. There desire clearly binds us to others still.[2] Our dependence on others is

[1] In such circumstances some form of aggression is a sign of life ; I do not say it is necessarily a practical or successful reaction, but as a psychological manifestation it is one move nearer to the fulfilment of the need than blank despair.

[2] It is interesting, though, that a strong psychological tendency is now manifesting itself to restrict and defy the force of love in erotic relations, and this is because such relations do involve to every individual some

manifestly a condition of our life in all its aspects :
self-preservative, sexual or pleasure-seeking. And
this means that some degree of sharing, some degree
of waiting, of giving up something for others, is
necessary in life. But though this brings a gain in
collective security, it can mean a loss of individual
security as well. So these dependent relationships
in themselves tend to rouse resistance and aggressive
emotions.

Now psycho-analysis can trace this anxiety of
dependence back through countless situations to
the very early one experienced by us all in babyhood—that of the child at the breast. A baby at the
breast is actually completely dependent on someone else, but has no fear of this, at least to begin
with, because he does not recognize his dependence.
In fact a baby does not recognize anyone's existence
but his own (his mother's breast is to him merely
a part of himself—just a sensation at first) and he
expects all his wants to be fulfilled. He (or she) wants
the breast for love of it, so to speak, for the pleasure
of sucking the milk, and also to still hunger. But what
happens if these expectations and wants are not
fulfilled ? In a certain degree the baby becomes
aware of his dependence ; he discovers that he
cannot supply all his own wants—and he cries and
screams. He becomes aggressive. He automatically
explodes, as it were, with hate and aggressive
craving. If he feels emptiness and loneliness, an
automatic reaction sets in, which may soon become

measure of compulsion and dependence. One type of
the present younger generation will not acknowledge
any feelings of *love*, even for a sexual partner or a child,
trying to base every human tie on reason alone, so
greatly is dependence feared by them.

uncontrollable and overwhelming, an aggressive rage which brings pain and explosive, burning, suffocating, choking bodily sensations ; and these in turn cause further feelings of lack, pain and apprehension. The baby cannot distinguish between ' me ' and ' not-me ' ; his own sensations are his world, *the* world to him ; so when he is cold, hungry or lonely there is no milk, no well-being or pleasure in the world—the valuable things in life have vanished. And when he is tortured with desire or anger, with uncontrollable, suffocating screaming, and painful, burning evacuations, the whole of his world is one of suffering ; it is scalded, torn and racked too. This situation which we all were in as babies has enormous psychological consequences for our lives.[1] It is our first experience of something like death, a recognition of the *non*-existence of something, of an overwhelming loss, both in ourselves and in others, as it seems. And this experience brings an *awareness of love* (in the form of desire), and a *recognition of dependence* (in the form of need), at the same moment as, and inextricably bound up with, feelings and uncontrollable sensations of *pain and threatened destruction* within and without. The baby's world is out of control ; a strike and an earthquake have happened in his world, and this is *because* he loves and desires, and such love may bring pain and devastation. Yet he cannot control or eradicate his desire or his hate, or his efforts to

[1] This psychological experience seems to be one of the peculiarities in man to which his evolutionary development has led. It is part of the same phenomenon as the long physical helplessness and dependence the human child goes through, as compared with other animals.

seize and obtain; and the whole crisis destroys his well-being.

The immediate reaction to this painful state of things is that he tries to regain, and also then to preserve, some measure of the blissful security he experienced before he felt the lack and his destructive impulses arose. Thus our great need develops for *security and safety* against these terrible risks and intolerable experiences of privation, insecurity and aggressions within and without. From such beginnings we all set out on our life-task of endeavouring to secure our self-preservation and our pleasures with the least possible risk of rousing destructive forces within ourselves, which may involve the destruction of others too.

Needless to say, neither these early emotional experiences, nor the adjustments that accompany and ensue from them, remain in our memories— our consciousness. The ' unconscious ' part of our minds is the territory of these feelings and of such experiences ; only a small part of the love, fear and hate that holds sway there all our lives ever becomes known to our conscious minds. Much of what I set out here, therefore, is always unconscious in us. Psycho-analysis might be described as the study of the motives of human behaviour, which have hitherto been so largely inexplicable because so largely unconscious, i.e. unknown to ourselves.

The hate and aggression, envy, jealousy and greed felt and expressed by grown-up people are all derivatives, and usually extremely complicated derivatives, both of this primary experience and of the necessity to master it if we are to survive and secure any pleasure at all in life. That is to say, however entirely aggressive and hateful these emotions in adult life may seem, they are in fact to some extent unconscious modifications and compromises of even simpler and cruder forms of these feelings. All our measures for achieving security are in addition bound up with a utilization in some way of love-impulses (the life-forces), though this too may at times appear only in very perverted and unrecognizable forms.

Projection

The first and the most fundamental of our insurances or safety-measures against feelings of pain, of being attacked, or of helplessness—one from which so many others spring—is that device we call projection. All painful and unpleasant sensations or feelings in the mind are by this device automatically relegated outside oneself ; one assumes that they belong elsewhere, not in oneself. We disown and repudiate them as emanating from ourselves ; in the ungrammatical but psychologically accurate phrase, we blame them *on* to someone else. In so far as such destructive forces are recognized in ourselves we claim that they have come there arbitrarily and by some external agency, and they should go back where they belong. To a baby, as I said, the differentiation between its pleasant and unpleasant states, good and bad feelings inside itself, is reflected on to the outside world and influences his differentiation between good and bad things and people in the world outside him. Projection is the baby's first reaction to pain, and it probably remains the most spontaneous reaction in all of us to any painful

feeling throughout our lives.[1] Subsequent mental
development enables each of us in a varying degree
to check or control this instantaneous primitive and
subjective reaction, and to substitute other methods
better adapted to the objective truth and reality
of the situation we are in.

The simplest example of projection in ordinary
life is the *Tu quoque*. If anyone attributes something
unpleasant to us, we often instantly assert that in
fact it is in him. But it happens even more often
without any provocation. We can see it as plain as
a pikestaff, for instance, in the ordinary man's
feelings about the wickedness and aggression of
other nations, but not of his own; or in his views
about the political party in opposition to his own.
What they do is dangerous, destructive and self-
seeking in the highest degree, while his own party's
intentions and motives are as pure and just as
fancy can make them. In their conditions of work,
quite ordinary men are prone to see selfish acquisi-
tiveness and ruthless aggressiveness either in their
employers or employees, whichever position they
do not hold themselves.

As an instance of the enormous strength and
universal functioning of this mechanism of projection, let me give the example of man's attitude
towards death. My argument is that we fear more
than anything else destructive forces operating

[1] This phenomenon occurs in fact not only with mental
feelings of an unpleasant kind, but is well known also
where physical pain is concerned. A man who was
given insufficient anæsthetic during a tooth-extraction
opened his eyes halfway through the process and saw
a *violent pain in the ceiling* ! The next second it was in his
mouth.

inside us against ourselves. Death represents the
farthest extreme of destructiveness that we can
conceive of, and one's own death of course represents the acme of inherent destructive forces operating *within* oneself. Now it is only within the last
two or three centuries of man's age-long history
that the fact of death has been widely acknowledged
as an inherent necessity, following on a destructive
process within our bodies. The primitive savage
regards death as sent by the will of an evil agency
outside him (demons), and in higher cultures the
will of a good external agency, God, has always
been held responsible for it. And even then the fact
of physical death has been denied by covering it,
so to speak, with a belief in our spiritual immor-
tality.

The first step in reassurance against dangers to
the self from within is thus made possible for us by
projection. Having in our own minds thus succeeded
in localizing and concentrating the danger outside us,
we then proceed to the next projective measure,
which consists in discharging the aggressive impulses
within us in an attack on this externally located
danger. Original aggression is expelled as a danger
and established elsewhere as something bad, and
then the object invested with dangerousness becomes a target at which aggression arising sub-
sequently can be discharged. As I said before,
aggression and hate boiling up within are felt in
the first instance to be uncontrollable ; they seem
to explode within us, and drown and burn and
suffocate our bodies in our first experience of them.
Later in life, too, people can feel like ' bursting ' with
rage, burning to seize what they want, itching to
tear out someone's eyes (or some other part of them),

or choking and suffocating with suppressed emotion. Then their minds seem to be put out of action and they cannot think or see or do the simplest things, much less work, or even, perhaps, for the time being look after their bodily safety. So we feel that, if all this is *not* to happen to us, such hate and rage must find a quick discharge elsewhere. A child who is full of hate against a loved person will hit another child or torture its dolls, or a man who is angry with his employer will curse his wife. As an old English proverb has it, ' The sack is beaten, but the ass is meant.' The savage belabours his idol when he is disappointed with the weather. We do this also by seeing evil in others who are far away, or at least at a safe distance from ourselves, whom we do not feel any need to love as we do those near us—such as foreigners, or capitalists, or perhaps prostitutes, or a specially hated race —some group whom people feel they may abominate if they like. These aggressive actions and attitudes are (especially to our unconscious minds) relatively *safe* methods of discharging hate and revenge, as compared with the simple original deepest form of such impulses: namely, the revengeful drive to rob and destroy someone on whom one depends, who may also at the same time be greatly loved and desired (in childhood to destroy the mother herself or the father and baby that she loves and owns as parts of herself).

We divide people into ' good ' and ' bad '— some we like and love, others we dislike or hate ; we try thus to isolate and *localize* these feelings and keep them from interfering with each other. This outlet also enables us to get *pleasure* by gratifying our aggressive feelings, without, we hope, incurring any corresponding damage to ourselves. So we provide ourselves with objects which can safely be made the targets of our aggression and hate, just as we provide ourselves with compartments and receptacles in our houses which can safely receive the offensive or injurious discharges of our bodies. Both these are typical ways, one psychological, the other physical, by which we strive to preserve to some degree the lives, health and sanity of ourselves and also of those we love and on whom we depend for our existence and our pleasures. And then we may let loose our hostility and hate on to these plague-spots we have ourselves brought into existence or helped to create. To take some very everyday examples: Think of the very common dislike children have of their cousins, especially when their relations with their own brothers and sisters are fairly good. The cousins become puppet brothers for the reception of what is in fact suppressed ' brotherly hate.' (It can happen conversely, too, that cousins receive the love denied to brothers and sisters.) And the children whom one's parents would like one to be friends with are as a rule cordially detested, mainly of course because one's parents like and approve of them, whereas parents are so often felt to do nothing but blame and interfere with oneself. Such ' nice ' children seem absolutely horrible!

All the feelings which originally attached to people can also be shifted and displaced on to things; this is another way of localizing feelings safely. As an instance, suppose a woman suddenly thinks her clothes are all ' hopeless ' and ' deadly,' worn out and ugly ; we see here, first, that her deepest fear that she has not enough life in her (or not

enough love, which is the psychological repre-
sentative of physical life) has caused her to feel
dependent on her clothes to make up the deficiency.
She has projected herself, or that part of her which
she unconsciously feels to be ' hopeless ' and
' deadly,' into them, and then attacks them as
enemies to herself and injurious to her. Next, perhaps, she induces her husband to provide her
with new clothes, and so finds some outlet against
him for her greediness and aggression ; but at the
same time she is saving him and herself from more
direct and dangerous expressions of it, from stealing
from him, or reproaching and nagging him, from
serious quarrels and the risk of a total loss of love
between them.

Distribution

In this mechanism we can see the enormous
importance that the factor of distribution in matters of love and hate has in the economics of our
emotional life, just as it has in the other economic
systems of human life. Our hate is distributed more
freely than our love, but is more suppressed at its
source—within ourselves—so that usually it escapes
in less volume and intensity. The explanation of
this is that, in those adults who are comparatively
normal and psychologically stable, a good proportion of their aggressive impulses becomes employed
inwardly, inside themselves, in opposing or checking
and regulating the flow, intensity and direction of
all emotions, whether loving and harmonizing or
vengeful and destructive.

This basic method of distributing and localizing
dangerous emotions has many offshoots. In the
first instance, as I explained, the angry child,

suffering from the destructive forces inside it, feels that the world outside, that is first of all his mother, is in the same state of anger and suffering. So it sees the evil things in itself as her, or a quality of her, not as a part or quality of itself. Hence good and bad states of feeling in the tiny child itself contribute largely to forming the foundation of its ideas of the world outside and of good and bad in that world. But sometimes they can entirely distort its perceptions of what is actually good and bad in its surroundings ; good can then be so greatly mistaken for bad and bad for good that no true sense of reality can be maintained, as in insanity. One way in which serious difficulties can arise here is that this first necessity to localize bad and painful things in the most loved and desired person may go too far, and lead on to an undue rejection of her and turning away from her.

Rejection

Now, some measure of *turning away* from a desired thing in order to find it more easily elsewhere is actually another basic mechanism of our psychological growth. Without some degree of dissatisfaction with our mother's milk and her nipples or with our bottles, we should none of us ever grow up mentally at all. By turning away, and also by subdividing our aims and distributing them elsewhere, the needs both of hunger and of sexual pleasure become detached from the mother. Food for the body and for pleasure of eating and drinking is gradually found elsewhere, while on turning away from the breast erotic pleasure also is rediscovered elsewhere.[1] We all go through this process. Either

[1] Erotic pleasure—gratification of bodily sensual

as baby girls we come to seek (and ultimately as
women to find) something like a mother's nipple
in the other sex, but something better than it—
better because then, as well as giving and receiving
pleasure, we can do something creative, something
which can bring life and happiness to another,
by means of what was originally sought for immediate
pleasure alone. Or as baby boys we turn away
from our mothers in a dissatisfaction which leads us
as it were, to split her in two and separate her nipple,
her milk-giving function, from herself. The nipple-
like organ with its fluid-producing functions the baby
boy soon finds on himself and keeps to use, to create
life and to give pleasure; the rest of his mother, her
body, her loving face, her encircling arms, he seeks
again elsewhere. So it is by turning away from our
mothers that we finally become, by our different
paths, grown men and women. Normally this is a
slow and gradual process of detachment from the
mother, but the acceptance of substitutes for her and
her breast can, even in babies, develop in an acute,
sudden and pathological way. A far too immediate

desires—is sought unconsciously by all of us throughout
life, and is consciously obtained in some form by most
of us throughout life. Adult sexual pleasure is the
adult—more developed—form of similar kinds of
gratification obtained earlier in life in other ways :
e.g. the baby at the breast gets sensual pleasure in
sucking the nipple at the same time as obtaining
needful sustenance. Psycho-analysis therefore describes
all such developmental forms of sexual pleasure as
' sexual ' ; because they all in fact contribute to the
building up of the final sexual capacity, and some of
them (such as sucking or sucking modified into kissing)
may even continue to play a direct part in adult sexual
activity.

and pronounced despairing rejection and withdrawal from her may take place, and also a deep and far-reaching *depreciation* of all much-loved and most-desired things.[1] In this way a loss of faith and belief in goodness itself can arise in certain people, which in part accounts for a tendency to distrust and avoid what they regard as good, as well as to hurt and destroy it out of disappointment and revenge. Turning away from something ardently desired and loved cannot be unmixed with hate and revenge ; though there are types of people, such as the kindly spinsters and friendly bachelors, who have disposed of this element of hate wonderfully well in their aversion from intimate contacts. In the miser and the recluse, however, we see that a dissatisfaction with the source of life has almost poisoned life itself for them, as they turned from it ; and their vindictive disappointment often vents itself in the few relations with the rest of the world they cannot avoid.

Depreciation and Contempt

This depreciation of the loved one, or of goodness, and loss of belief in it, is familiar to us all in the story of the fox and the ' sour grapes.' In its way it can be a useful and widespread mechanism for enabling us to bear disappointments without becoming savage. In everyday life it may be very

[1] A certain degree of depreciation of any loved person or thing that has been renounced is probably inevitable, even if it be little more than an awakening to the fact that the desired one had been too greatly idealized. But in the unconscious this depreciation is often strong and persists permanently, though it may be carefully masked in conscious attitudes.

convenient to a woman and her husband if she never likes the look of anything in an expensive shop. But this reaction has great dangers ; such a woman will often be mean, carping and over-critical in regard to other matters, especially in personal relations. ' Sour grapes ' and the method of turning away in contempt from what we really admire and desire does not make for greater good-will in the world generally. Suppose, instead, that a woman looks at a shop full of expensive things which she cannot afford, without buying any, but ad-miring and wishing for the best and ignoring what is unattractive. She will thus have employed *inwardly*, in curbing and restraining her wishes, the strength of her disappointment and revengeful feelings (her aggression), to enable her to go without the desired thing. She has turned her aggression (towards what she cannot get) against herself and her own desires to get. In this way she will have been generous with love, though not wasteful with money, *outwardly*. The former over-critical type of woman, on the other hand, does not turn her aggression inwards against herself, and engage in an inner struggle to curb her desires. She is still using a more primitive method of ridding herself of them, by directing her hate out-ward, spoiling what she wants in her own eyes, and so ceasing to like (love) and want it. It is a simpler method, less complicated and more immediately pleasurable to herself than the inner struggle to curb desire, but less advantageous in the long run either to herself or to the rest of the community. Hate is turned outward instead of love, and is used to avert and cover up love, so that in the end less love and more hate comes into play in life.

Turning away in contempt or rejection from a desired object can be a dangerous psychological reaction, if it is not used merely as a restraint on greed, and especially if revenge and retaliation inspire it as well. The most impressive evidence of this may be seen when such a reaction leads to suicide—when disappointment and the fury of revenge engender such hatred and contempt of life and all it offers that life itself is finally rejected and destroyed.

The reaction of contempt and rejection is also probably the biggest motive and main source of all the countless varieties of faithlessness, betrayal, desertion, infidelity and treachery so constantly manifested in life, particularly by special types of people in whom this mechanism is strongly pronounced—from the Don Juans or the prostitutes (in sexual matters) to the rolling stones who never keep to one job or one line of work (in self-preservative matters). Such people spend their lives seeking, then finding, then being disappointed because their desires are inordinate and unrealizable either in quality or degree ; ultimately they turn away, spurn and reject—only to start the search instantly all over again.

Let me remind you here of the aim—the unconscious teleological principle, if you like—at work behind all these various modes of reaction and behaviour, these various adaptations and adjustments, or maladjustments, that I am describing. This aim is that of dealing with and disposing of our dangerous and destructive feelings in such a way that we obtain the maximum security in life and pleasure too. In my last illustration—the Don Juans in the field of love and the rolling stones in the field of work—we can see fairly clearly the main methods used, because they are so crude and exaggerated. We see how the insatiable longings of such people, which are not very different at bottom from simple inordinate greed, cause them inevitably to become dissatisfied and discontented with whatever they get, thus arousing their fear of dependence, revenge and aggression and threatening their own safety and peace of mind, besides that of the woman or whoever disappoints them. All the evil impulses in themselves—the hate, greed and revengeful disappointment—they then expel psychologically into the person or work from whom they had expected so much, and perceive it all there ; and then naturally feel it both necessary and justified to turn away and flee from that person or work.

Now flight is essentially and invariably a safety device; and we must consider what it is that is *saved* by rejection. Fundamentally, life is saved by it, since such people feel threatened on all sides as they are ; but more than this, they are trying to secure their pleasure too. As I described, to each of us as tiny babies, goodness, pleasure and satisfaction were all one and the same thing, identical— all three experienced in one sensation, a good feeling in body and mind alike, a heavenly content. And they remain thus united in the depths, up to the last breath we draw, in spite of the complications and distinctions that we consciously make between them later. In fleeing from a good thing which has become more or less bad in our eyes, we are—in our minds—*preserving* a vision of goodness which had almost been lost ; for by discovering it elsewhere we seem, as it were, to bring it to life again in another place.

We try to make a fantastic ' reparation ' by acclaiming the goodness unharmed elsewhere. The Don Juans and rolling stones too retain their longing for goodness—such goodness as they can recognize ; and they start every time on their old search for a greater security or greater pleasure in love or sexual satisfaction than they have ever found or ever will find. In their flights one can see an interaction of love and hate impulses. Rejection can even be a method of loving, distorted indeed, but aiming at the preservation of something unconsciously felt to be ' too good for me.' Desertion then ' saves ' the goodness thus recognized, spares it and rescues it from one's own worthlessness, which could ruin it. Sometimes this love in it predominates, as in certain suicides, when that supreme instance of self-withdrawal represents to the clouded mind a gift of one's life to ensure the happiness of another. In such a case the same sharp differentiation and separation of good and bad states that I described in discussing projection has been carried out, but in the converse direction. Such a suicide has localized all badness and evil in himself, where he intends it to die with him, and has concentrated all his own desires, hopes and aspirations for goodness outside him, in the loved person for whose sake, according to his confused perceptions, he feels he is renouncing all that is good, together with life itself.

The need to rediscover goodness elsewhere, as well as to separate it from hate and danger, can thus lead to continual fresh starts; and, whereas in certain types this device becomes over-developed, it is employed to some extent by all ordinary stable people. The man who lives with his parents all his life and never seeks work or a wife away from home is perhaps in one way even less normal than a sexual rake. The impulse to a fresh start, in a mild form, is really one great motive behind a very important phenomenon in human life, so important that it has been regarded by some observers as an instinct in itself and called the herd instinct. Man's need for the society of his fellows is of course no simple manifestation, and every single element and every mechanism in his psychology will be found to contribute to it ; but it is probably true that where this impulse is strongly developed it represents more particularly the need to collect and accumulate a specially large measure of love, support and so *security*, which will be available as a perpetual reserve to be drawn upon at need. I said before that hate can be used to avert or cover up desire or love. Now most especially gregarious and ' popular ' people are using love to avert hate and its dangers. Such people make a collection of friends, so that if one fails them they will still never be without. Moreover, to have friends and to be liked proves to them that they themselves are good, i.e. that the dangerousness in them is non-existent or safely disposed of. Thus by collecting goodness all round them, which they can dip into at any moment, they re-create for themselves (by their unconscious phantasy-attitude) a kind of substitute mother's breast which is always at their disposal and never frustrates or fails them. This cardinal phantasy of an ever-bountiful never-failing breast is naturally the defence *par excellence* against the possibility of feelings either of destitution or destructiveness arising in oneself. It is of course worked out in many other ways besides the one of accumulating hosts of friends ; it is what the man meant who said ' the world was his oyster.' The essence of the phantasy is that what we want we can get, and then we feel secure against the danger of the emptiness and destructiveness which arise if we cannot get. But such a need can have its greedy aspects and it often implies little self-sufficiency, little self-confidence beneath, in one's capacity to secure or to produce a sufficiency of the good things of life. Those who seek most from others in fact seldom give much to others.

Popularity, social success, gregariousness and so on, besides their many other uses and significances, are also wider and more generalized forms of similar behaviour in definitely sexual attachments, such as the tendency to have many love-affairs either at one time or successively. It is a case of collecting innumerable eggs in different baskets ; the danger of frustration and failure is lessened, and the risk of one's own greed or cruelty wasting and ruining the prized good thing or loved person is reduced by subdivision of one good into many. There is a strong feeling that a loss inflicted on a large number will be so small to each member of that number as to be negligible ; and an outlet of a relatively safe kind is obtained for the discharge and satisfaction of aggression, as well as a safeguard against its effects.

Envy

This need to secure oneself against loss or danger within and without induces some people to accumulate and store up all the good they can lay hold of, and this may well lead round again to *envy* in

the perpetual circle of desire, frustration and hate—
unless it can ascend into a spiral by bringing in
more love. For as soon as the need for *much* is
strong, it is clear that comparisons have begun to
enter in. Now a comparison between ourselves and
others is no primary simple situation in itself. It
is, however, a more developed and complicated
version of the primary situation I described earlier,
when the baby feels the *difference* between pleasant
good states of well-being in itself and painful
dangerous feelings and states. All comparisons
began with that comparison. The immediate urge
is to reinstate the condition of well-being. Since
to a baby well-being comes principally by means of
its mouth and by milk, the process of taking in and
getting acquires great significance to us as a means
of warding off or ousting pain and the dangers
of consequent aggressive feelings. This impulse to
take in something good in order to increase the feeling
of inner well-being links up with the mental process
known as introjection—a correlate of projection,
which is the process of psychically expelling into the
outside world whatever is felt as bad and harmful in
us. Whether or not constitutional differences exist in
the strength of the acquisitive impulse in individuals,
there can be no doubt that an accentuation of the
desire to take in, as a defence against disintegration
within, is an important factor wherever greed is at
all marked. The connection of greed and acquisi-
tiveness with *security* is in any case evident.

Greed

Some measure of greed exists unconsciously in
everyone. It represents an aspect of the desire to
live, one which mingled and fused at the outset

of life with the impulse to turn aggression and destructiveness outside ourselves against others, and as such it persists unconsciously throughout life. By its very nature it is endless and never assuaged ; and being a form of the impulse to live, it ceases only with death.

The longing or greed for good things can relate to any and every imaginable kind of good— material possessions, bodily or mental gifts, advantages and privileges ; but, beside the actual gratification they may bring, in the depths of our minds they all ultimately signify one thing. They stand as proofs to us, if we get them, that we are ourselves good, and full of good, and so are worthy of love, or respect and honour, in return. Thus they serve as proofs and insurances against our fears of the emptiness inside ourselves, or of our evil impulses which make us feel bad and full of badness to ourselves and others. They also defend us against our fear of the retaliation, punishment or retribution which may be carried out against us by others, whether in material or in moral ways, or in our affections and love-relations. One great reason why a *loss* of any kind can be so painful is that unconsciously it represents the converse idea, that we are being exposed as *unworthy* of good things, and so our deepest fears are realized. When a person, whose sense of security is largely based on his greed—on the feeling that he has, or can get, as much as he needs of good things—sees that someone else has more than he, it upsets this self-protective edifice of security ; he feels reduced to poverty, as if he had little—' too little good '—in him. Not only has his unconscious protective defence vanished, but he feels in phantasy as if the others who have more must have actually *robbed* him of what had made him feel secure, which now is gone. That is why the feeling of envy is so exceedingly poignant and bitter to those who experience it. They feel they are being forced to submit to robbery and persecution!

Delusional Hate

It is easy to see that this unconscious belief or suspicion—that others who possess more than oneself have acquired it through robbing oneself—though so illogical, is amazingly soothing. For it throws the responsibility for feelings of poverty and worthlessness, especially for poverty in love and goodwill, on to other people ; and it brings absolution of all guilt, greed or selfishness towards them, for *they* are the cause that one is ' no good in the world.' Feelings of grudge and grievance too—the idea that ' nobody helps *me* '—develop as a projection from an unconscious knowledge of one's own laziness and meanness towards others. This projection, when it gets too strong a hold and is not checked by goodwill and insight, is the kernel of most forms of delusional insanity, in which other people are felt to be robbing, poisoning, or conspiring against one.

There is a delusional jealousy, too ; envy and jealousy are indeed very closely allied. The jealous person always feels he is being robbed of his loved one. The feeling that one is being robbed only becomes delusional, however, when there is such a deep and radical doubt and despair about one's own powers and capacities for love and goodness that one feels absolutely at the mercy of the evil in oneself and lacking in any means to counteract it.

That is a feeling that fortunately most of us rarely experience, except perhaps when we have suffered real and serious losses, such as the death of people we love. This unconscious feeling of our own utter worthlessness (in not having done more for the loved one) is part of the experience of grief.

We tend to think of envy as a natural or inevitable feeling ; but the fact remains that strong feelings of envy are characteristic of some people and not of others, whatever their circumstances. We all know the really envious type of person, who has a perpetual look of discontented agitation and suffering, whose sharp eyes seem to be registering comparisons ceaselessly, and who can think of nothing but what they have *not* got. Yet actually such people are often a great deal better off, in material ways, than most of those in their near surroundings. When envy reaches such a point as this, the wheel has come a bit too far round in the circle; for instead of being able to get and acquire more for themselves and enjoy the satisfaction and security of good fortune, their sense of danger (derived from their own greediness) is so strong that they have to protest and declare that they have nothing : that is, that they have *not* been guilty of greediness, of seizing and storing up for themselves and robbing others of good things to enrich themselves. One common type is that of a person who, though always envious, never makes any effort to acquire or obtain anything, and never tries to succeed in any way. Here one sees clearly that both the envy and the lack of success are proving to him that he is not actually taking from others. Though this psychological attitude serves well enough the purpose of giving security and reassurance against fear, it is a pathological development and does not make them satisfactory people, even to themselves. For one thing, spending so much time and energy as they do in feeling deprived and frustrated in life, envious people have little or none left for any direct enjoyment. Indirect enjoyment they get in feeling deprived and injured by others. There is an aggressive sadistic pleasure in disparaging and discrediting the others who have more, though it may be only indirectly expressed ; it also contains a very hidden and distorted kind of love, in their *not taking* anything good for themselves and in restricting themselves to wishing and envying.

Envy of the Other Sex

One of the most important varieties of envy in human life, and one we are usually very little aware of, is the envy we all unconsciously feel to some extent of members of the opposite sex. Except in the way in which it becomes conscious in women who feel that men have various advantages they want, and except in men whose erotic life is consciously homosexual, this envy is, practically speaking, never recognized. Yet some degree of it exists in everyone ; and it can be of great strength unconsciously without being suspected by the person concerned. Where the bisexual attitudes have not become fully integrated and woven together in the fabric of the whole personality— where the male and female attitudes merely alternate or conflict—other people at least will perceive something of their original simple significance ; they will think that ' Miss or Mrs. Smith is a masculine type of woman,' or that Mr. Robinson is rather ' weak ' or has some feminine trait, such as exhibitionism perhaps. This kind of envy is an enormous topic ; the little I can say here cannot do justice to it. Obviously a sense of lack and a wish for something more than one has is a strong component in it. In the depths of the mind, and in small children, the wish does actually relate to something one literally does not possess, to parts of the body and functions that one will never have. Girls envy boys and men their penis and what they can do with it, directing their urine with it, or putting it into women and giving them babies, and so on.

Women's envy of men relates to all their various kinds of ' potency ' in life, e.g. their physical strength and intellectual powers. Those women who envy men keenly constantly seek for and enjoy any demonstration that they can do what men can, which means that they do not lack any organ or function men have, brain or skill, wherewith to perform special tasks. And I think the man's capacity for initiative and enterprise, which is based so much on self-confidence, is especially envied by women. Men are more confident than women on the whole. The man has an external sexual organ he can see and he knows that it functions. Women can obtain less direct reassurance of this kind about their capacities. Girls have to wait many years for it ; not till the man has played his part and till a child is born can they gain absolute proof of their sexual capacities ; and even then their value in their own eyes may be so much bound up with the perfection of their children as to be in constant jeopardy.

Even yet it is often not realized how much boys envy girls, and especially envy women (their

mothers) for their breasts and milk, and above all
for the mysterious capacity women's bodies have of
forming and creating babies out of food and what
men give them. Both boys and girls tend to feel
that *their* bodies can only form fæces and urine and
that they can only produce that kind of material.
Most of the ordinary activities of both sexes are
normally capable of unconsciously expressing both
male and female functions in co-operation. Men's
desire for female functions comes openly to expression in painters and writers, who feel they give
birth to their works like a woman in labour after
long pregnancy. All artists, in whatever medium,
in fact work largely through the feminine side of
their personalities ; this is because works of art
are essentially formed and created inside the mind
of the maker, and are hardly at all dependent on
external circumstances. In contrast, the practical
man working in a practical world on matters
external, more independent of his own imaginings,
is typically expressing a more masculine function.

These desires to possess the advantages of the other
sex in addition to one's own are a very useful element
in character-formation : indeed, no one can be
regarded as fully developed unless the bisexual or
homosexual side of his character is finding an outlet
in some sublimated and thus productive form. It
is only when the desires for good things, and for
more than one has, have become attached in the
mind *exclusively* to the attributes or advantages of
the other sex and no substitutes will be accepted
that this envy becomes unmanageable or pathological. It is only when people have despaired,
at any rate relatively speaking, and abandoned
hope of getting satisfaction or security from the

functions and opportunities specifically belonging to
their own sex, that they develop an intense and
bitter envy of the other. When a little girl has come
unconsciously to fear the destructive impulses
inside herself so much that she doubts if she could
ever produce anything but corrupt and offensive
stuff (like bad fæces), and feels that even if she could
get hold of a baby-seed safely—without guilt and
without damaging and robbing a brother, or her
father and mother, by so doing—and feels that her
own inside may be so full of badness that the baby
would surely die—when she feels all this she turns in
dread away from that side of life and develops a masculine role. She is thus voluntarily, though not consciously, making a sacrifice of her feminine hopes and
wishes, and without necessarily losing the large
admixture of love which is bound up with her
adoption of a masculine role. She not only refrains
from the feminine acts by which she feels she
would harm all those she loved, but remains un-
married and perhaps devotes herself to looking
after her parents or brothers and sisters, and making
reparation to them. She has to get some compensation for these sacrifices, however, and she draws this
from her envy of men. The unconscious psychological value of her envy consists again of its significance as a protest, reassurance, and security to
her. As long as she envies men she won't have a
baby or be exposed to those terrible risks at all.
She is proving that she never wanted feminine
satisfactions, never wanted her mother's husband
and babies, nor imitated her parents in ' making
babies ' with other children, which she felt was
seducing and corrupting them and also trying
to get things that she had no right to. By throwing

the accent on a masculine way of life, which she also desires in itself, she protests that she is not greedy for men and babies, and is neither harming men nor, through her greed, robbing other women of the love of men. Thus she gets a security against her worst fears; and she may look for satisfaction to the other side of her nature and develop her wish to be a man.

Men's envy of women is not less common than women's of men, nor less profound. But it is much less recognized and understood; and I think this is due, not simply to the prejudice of men on this delicate point, but to the nature of things. As far as a little boy's envy of his mother's breasts and milk is concerned, he has himself a special organ to set off against them, a penis. Now his little sisters have not got either penis or breasts; so that his satisfaction and superiority about having a penis can be used to conceal and counterbalance his wish for a body which could make and feed babies. All their lives men continue to make use of this compensation against their envy of women, and one important element in the enormous psychological significance of the penis is to be found in this compensation. The chief reason why men's envy of women remains so hidden is because it relates precisely to the *inside* of women's bodies, to the mysterious functions and processes that go on, magically, as it seems, inside women (their mothers), making babies and milk. It appears too that, just as women envy men's initiative, conversely men envy women's capacity for passive experience, especially the capacity to bear and to suffer. Suffering relieves guilt; especially is the pain that brings life into the world doubly enviable unconsciously to men.

Men cannot easily become conscious of what they envy, because they do not really altogether know what it is. Woman has always been said to be an enigma by men ; many men have a slightly superstitious feeling of awe about a pregnant woman. Their speculations and imaginings about the experiences of women are of course part of their phantasy-life, which they usually keep very much apart from their conscious everyday life; there they naturally prefer only to show their masculine side, since that they both know about and can use. It would seem that, prejudice apart, we have to employ a special technique for exploring the unconscious mind before we can obtain access to the sources and understanding of that strong envy in men of women, which lies hidden in the life of imagination and phantasy.

In psycho-analytic work one comes across phantasies and anxiety-situations in men which throw a strong light on some primitive rites and customs among savages, and clearly establish that their origin lies partly in the envy of women felt by men. One of these is the ' couvade,' the custom by which a man whose wife is in childbirth goes to bed and is treated exactly like his wife during the whole period of lying-in. In analysis there come to light in men wishes and phantasies to undergo a state of couvade, or symptoms which in effect cause them to do so at such times. These wishes and symptoms prove to be largely due to envy of their wives for being able to produce a live child and for being so much admired and treated as so important on account of it. But further, one also sees that where the envy is so strong, the sense of guilt and unworthiness in the man is correspondingly strong underlying the envy and partly causing it. A man's deep fear of the strength of destructiveness and greedy savagery in himself towards his wife and children (originally towards his mother and her other children) strengthens his envy of his wife's productivity and her more directly demonstrable capacity to create and bring life into the world.

Rivalry

The impulse towards competitiveness, and rivalry in general, is drawn from many interacting sources, self-preservative, sexual, and aggressive. Some degree of it is of course a generally normal and useful character-trait. When it is severely inhibited we find deep hidden in the mind a defeatist attitude. The person does not trust himself to struggle with others, or win, without doing them irreparable harm, and without being punished severely himself for risking such harm to them. Over-development of competitiveness can lead to great suffering of mind and constant unpleasantness in human relations, although it can be the source of considerable achievement. Rivalry is on the whole productive in character when it does not go too far. One very often sees, however, that though it may give great temporary satisfaction, ' success ' brings no peace of mind or security. How often great or eminent people dare not tolerate any but mediocre people round them ; and how common it is for men of exceptional ability and parts to choose particularly dull, plain, or even useless wives, and *vice versa*. Let me take one special type of rivalry often seen ; we hear of the prima donna, for instance, who, however good her voice, will not sing in opera with any other first-rate singer. In addition to the material, sexual and acquisitive satisfactions her voice brings her, the *superiority* of her voice over others' has become her chosen way of feeling secure, and is her insurance against the fear of evil in herself leading to helpless isolation and a sense of death. Consequently such people are for ever trying to be placed in a sharp contrast with inferior mortals, in order unfailingly to be acclaimed good and admirable, and in order to feel constantly that others are bad and not they. In a milder form this is an exceedingly common character-trait ; many people are really happy and contented only with those in some way inferior to themselves—it may be intellectually, or by class standards, or even morally inferior. These inferior ones are the people they really need and are dependent on in life. Those who need inferiors to consort with are of course the converse of snobs, but both they and the snobs seek the same thing at heart in different ways. Both need a reassurance and a guarantee that they are not poor, mean and empty, unworthy and unlovable themselves.

In all these situations where projection is used, and other people are regarded as bad instead of oneself, it will be clear that the villain of the piece, the rival or whoever it may be who is serving us as a receptacle for our own dangerous and unwanted features, actually becomes to us unconsciously the evil part of ourselves, the ' double ' of that side of us. This process is often very clear in drama and literature, where such personifications form the stock-in-trade of the writer. Iago, for instance, represents Othello's own greedy impulses, which also are subtly indicated in the unconscious symbolic significance of Othello's blackness.

Once we see evil in someone else it becomes possible and may seem necessary to let loose pent-up aggression against that person. It is here that the large part played in life by condemnation of others, criticism, denunciation, and intolerance generally, comes in. What we cannot tolerate in ourselves we are not likely to tolerate in others. In so condemning others we can obtain gratification, too, both directly from discharging our aggressive impulses, and from the reassurance obtained that we ourselves conform to and uphold the standards of rightness and perfection. Righteous indignation can be one of the cruellest and most vindictive of aggressive pleasures. This very important expression of aggressive impulses in civilized life is seen in countless everyday situations ; it is the object of every dispute to prove oneself right, but very commonly the principal immediate object is really to prove the other fellow wrong. Religious persecution is founded on this mechanism, and so are the fulminations of the leader-writer and orator ; most of the animus in political life, and a good deal of the destructive work done in scientific societies, derives from nothing else—so do the recriminations of lovers and married couples. It is interesting to compare this attitude of intolerance with that of the last type of people I mentioned, who one may say are too tolerant of imperfections or unworthiness in their companions. Both, however, achieve the same end by different routes, a utilization of some form of dependence for a gain in the security of peace of mind.

Love of Power

One emotional attitude containing a marked element of aggression is the love of power, or the

' will to power.' It is of immense psychological
importance, but too complicated to be discussed
in detail here. Broadly speaking, it derives from
the attempt to control the dangers in oneself more
directly than by the methods of projection and of
flight. It is always the *uncontrollable* character of
one's desire and aggression, and one's *helplessness*
in face of these impulses, that is most dreaded.
One way of reaching security is by aiming at
omnipotent power in order to control all potentially
painful conditions, and have access to all useful,
desirable things, both within oneself and without.
In phantasy, omnipotence shall bring security.
The manifestations of our attempts at omnipotence
are legion ; and some degree of it is implied in all
the other forms of aggression and the defences against
the dangers of dependence or extinction that I have
described. Power is not necessarily even indirectly
aggressive, but it has a strong tendency to become so.
One form of omnipotence as a means of obtaining
security consists in experimenting, as it were, with
danger, in order to *test* one's power of escape. The
ultimate danger such people dread is actually the
retribution and persecution they unconsciously
expect from all those loved and hated persons whom
their greed in thought or deed has injured. People
in whom the will to power as a method of attaining
security is over-developed may of course become
dictators; but they may also become criminals,
gangsters, road-hogs and so on. They occupy their
lives with testing whether or not they can escape
the retribution of, for instance, accidents, prison,
and even the gallows.

Naturally, in the dangers of economic depression,
with all the disruption and destruction they may

bring, lies the opportunity of tyrants. When such a one has climbed ruthlessly upon the shoulders of men more tender or more timid than himself, he may attempt to prove that he can be stronger than the danger of economic disaster and will hope to show himself as the saviour of the situation. Incidentally, starting a war in another (perhaps distant) country, and thus deflecting or localizing the disruptive forces, is quite typical of omnipotent self-defensive measures.

There may be attempts too at omnipotent control by love ; some leaders of religion would favour this. But the power of love is a fundamentally different thing from the love of power, which is essentially egoistic and cannot amalgamate with love to any degree ; it can only simulate it. Genuine love denotes a capacity for sacrifice, some endurance of pain, some dependence—for the sake of love, a greater gain ; the need for power springs directly from an incapacity to tolerate either sacrifices for others or dependence on others. Because of this underlying incapacity any attempt to achieve an apparently constructive aim by excessive omnipotence is always false—based on a fallacy—and succeeds, if it is a 'success,' only by trickery or violence.

It is not possible for me to discuss here many important aspects of my subject, such as the insidious and indirect expressions of hate and aggression ; treachery, hypocrisy, misrepresentation, lying, fraud, and so on ; nor the allied forms such as meanness, the refusing and withholding of love or generosity in various ways.[1]

[1] This omission is by no means intended to represent them as of secondary importance ; in fact they are insufficiently recognized or understood, and greatly underestimated. But in this short study I am obliged

Jealousy

Jealousy is not nearly such a simple reaction as we assume, even though we regard it as so ' natural '; indeed it is often felt when it is not in fact justified by circumstances. The typical situation of jealousy is of course that of rivalry in love. You will expect me here to refer to the Œdipus complex and to say that all jealousy derives from that first experience of sexual rivalry in our childhood. You are right ; but that is not enough as an explanation. We do of course repeat the experiences of our childhood ever after, more or less ; but individuals vary even in this ; and we do not repeat our infantile experiences for the mere fun of repeating them, so to speak. When we do, it is for the same reason that we behaved in that way in the first instance, and because, although we have grown older, we have not yet found a better way.

In so far as jealousy is a reaction of hate and aggression to a loss or threat of a loss, it is simple and primary enough, and as inevitable as any such reaction on this pattern. But one special feature in jealousy is the sense of humiliation which invariably accompanies it, owing to the injury it entails to one's self-confidence and sense of security. The loss of self-confidence is not always consciously felt by a jealous person. If you reflect, you will see that the more furious and aggressive he is the less humiliated he feels ; and *vice versa*, the less aggressive and angry, the more miserable and low-spirited he is. The jealous person inevitably feels humiliated and inferior, and, less consciously, unworthy,

to confine myself to considering open forms of aggression —the simpler and more familiar manifestations of my subject.

depressed and guilty. The explanation of this is that if he is not loved, or thinks he is not, it unconsciously signifies to him that he is *not lovable*, that he is hateful, full of hate. Unconsciously or not, he feels it was because he was not good enough to her that he has been deserted or neglected by the one he loves. The depression and feeling of helpless exposure to danger which this thought of being unlovable rouses in him (with all the fears of loneliness that accompany it) are unendurable. This explains the poignancy and torturing bitterness of jealousy, and this we all endeavour to relieve by condemning and hating someone else, in this case the rival. The realization of dependence has come back from earliest childhood with all its dangers and the wheel begins to revolve again as it did in babyhood. Projection is at once set in motion. Evil and destructiveness is seen in a rival, he is condemned, and hate can be let loose against him without a sense of guilt.

It is probable that our need in babyhood to project our dangerous painful states of anger out of us into someone else and identify someone else with them, and ourselves only with our good states, is one of the main stimuli towards recognizing other people's existence at all. In other words, our whole interest in the outer world and other people is ultimately founded on our need of them ; and we need them for two purposes. One is the obvious one of getting satisfactions from them, both for our self-preservative and pleasure needs. The other purpose for which we need them is to hate them, so that we may expel and discharge our own badness, with its dangers, out of ourselves on to them. That, I think, is why jealousy is so often felt where it is unfounded. When anyone—unconsciously—feels himself deficient in love and goodness, and fears that this deficiency may be discovered and exposed by his love-partner, or may hurt her, then he begins to be jealous and to *look for* lack of love in that partner, so as not to see it in himself, and to see wickedness in a rival instead of in himself.

Incidentally, this accusation—' *You* don't love *me* ! '—is the burden of every lovers' quarrel and of the unhappiness young wives and husbands often go through before they ' settle down,' as old-fashioned people called it. The misery, feelings of guilt, the expiation in remorse and tears, and the absolution of forgiveness reached in the end all display very clearly that an unconscious feeling of unlovableness and unworthiness in oneself is what sets this familiar process of quarrelling going.

Now the man who has lost the woman he loves, or thinks he will lose her, is reacting not only to the loss of her love or his possession of her, but also to the loss of them as proofs of his own value to himself, and so of his own security, in the world of his own mind, to say nothing of the outside world. His value to himself may be represented by strength, intellect, sexual potency, moral virtues, wealth—any of a legion of symbols of goodness, which vary with each individual but in each case represent that individual's chosen insurances, as it were, his resources in himself to counterbalance and safeguard him against the dangers of evil forces within him. A sexual partner—and to most people especially in the settled relation of marriage, where there is some responsibility and obligation on both sides—is felt to be a great recognition, and thus a proof, of that preponderance of good over evil in ourselves that we all seek, and on which our peace of mind depends.

It would be interesting to consider marriage in civilized life from this point of view alone ; how much does this motive of the need for reassurance about one's own value play a part in the decisions of men and women to marry, and how little in comparison with it does the feeling of love or sexual desire impel them ? Without psycho-analysing them, it would be impossible to estimate these different factors in the more normal individuals. For true love, as we call it, is precisely a condition in which the two factors coalesce and become indistinguishable, in which ease of mind and happiness are perpetually being derived from the fact that the man or woman is full of a love which can satisfy and fulfil the needs even of another beside himself. A mutual love serves as a double insurance to each partner. The other's love, added to one's own, doubles one's store of love and well-being and so of insurance against pain, destructiveness and inner destitution ; and also, in complementing and fulfilling each other's sexual needs, each transforms the sexual desire of the other from a potential pain and source of destructiveness in him or her, to an absolute pleasure and source of well-being. By this partnership in love, therefore, satisfaction of the harmonizing and unifying life-instincts, the self-preservative and sexual, is gained ; and security against the destructive impulses and the dangers of loss, loneliness, and helplessness is increased. A benign circle of enjoyment with a minimum of privation and aggression has been achieved and the *advantages of dependence* are being used to the full. Even so, pleasure in safe and constructive forms of aggression must be obtained somewhere to a sufficient degree. Where the anxiety and distrust of others arising from too much projection is at all intense, the dependence in marriage will give rise to accessions of fear and hate, which destroy all possibility of a benign love-circle, and set up a vicious circle of greed, frustration and disintegration again.

Conscience, Morality and Love

It will appear that I have said very little about guilt, and have hardly mentioned those important subjects, hate of oneself and aggression turned against the self in painful inner struggles. A large part of our aggression is taken up and concentrated into that part or function of the self called in modern psychology the super-ego[1]—the active principles and standards within us—which unconsciously dictates a great deal of our behaviour, and often handles the self proper with great severity. So far as we are aware of this part of ourselves and its influence on us, we call it conscience ; one reason why a large part of this function lies outside consciousness is because there are strong motives in us to suppress and ignore a side of ourselves which may cause pain to us and which also attempts to interfere with many of our gratifications.

I have tried to show that we spend our lives in the task of attempting to keep a sort of balance

[1] For the development of this psycho-analytical concept the reader is referred to the works of Sigm. Freud, *The Ego and the Id* ; *Group Psychology* ; and *Collected Papers* : ' Narcissism,' ' Mourning and Melancholia,' etc. (Selections from the above are contained in *Psycho-Analytical Epitome* No. 1.)

between the life-bringing and the destructive elements in ourselves. Conscience is really nothing but the peak, penetrating into our conscious minds, of our unconscious realization of the necessity to fulfil this task. In the depths and beneath some apparent contradictions, what conscience decrees is always guided by the principle of checking impulses which lead to destructiveness. One reason why sexual impulses are felt so strongly to be guilty is because they are apt to be so imperative, i.e. aggressive and selfish, that they may cause harm to ourselves or others.[1] Conscience, as we know it, has only one discipline—do this, the productive thing ; don't do that, the destructive thing. It is but another word for a self-control which should keep a proper balance between egoism and altruism, and between love and hate.

One institution, evolved by humanity as an aid, broadly speaking, in controlling hate and egoism, has existed since immemorial times—I mean religion—however inadequately the various forms of it may have fulfilled the task. The ' desire for goodness ' originally (in our babyhood) stirred greed and aggression as well as love and tenderness in us. In the early forms of religion this association was still apparent ; ' goodness,' the God, was killed and eaten as well as worshipped and adored.

---

[1] A sexual act performed in order to create a child, i.e. to bring something into life, is to some people far more justifiable than any other. This is because the conscious intention of it assuages conscience and allays guilt—the guilt that relates to the aggression in sexuality. The deepest reason why sexuality is so guilty is that our earliest sexual desires were in fact closely bound up with impulses of hate and destructiveness.

There had been several religious movements aiming at a separation of these two tendencies before the Christian era; the one that emerged as Christianity, and became one of the great religions of the world, was very largely a supreme endeavour to dissociate all aggression and greed from love. It attempted this by exalting altruistic love to an ideal, but at the same time by denying the reality of many problems that are part of the soul's life—of man's psychology. His aggressive and sexual impulses, if their existence was not altogether denied, were despised and condemned, or ignored. This denial is not peculiar to Christianity, nor have the best interpreters of that religion subscribed to it. It was and is a general tendency in man to deny and ignore what he fears in himself;[1] Christianity, however, adopted and in some ways specially represented the tendency, thus encouraging and maintaining it.

But aggression and sexuality, being integral parts of human nature, are bound to function, for either good or ill, while life lasts. If the attempt is made to deny their rights and exclude them from participation in life for good, they must flow into channels of hate and destructiveness. In such forms as persecution, rapacity, asceticism and pharasaism —the inevitable accompaniments of such a dissociation—they forced their way back into the life of religion and harassed the lives of men. Moreover, because Christianity limited goodness so largely to an altruistic attitude in the emotions and *within the mind*, and denied the importance of the external material world, the aggression it denied also had to

[1] I referred to this method of denial explicitly on p. 20 and implicitly in many passages.

find its outlet in a *personal* way, e.g. in proselytism and persecution against the beliefs, and ultimately against the persons, of men and women. Aggression had no opportunity for expression in the impersonal ways which offer great constructive outlets for it: in the intellectual sphere, or against nature in practical enterprises such as exploration or experimentation. These worldly fields of effort were regarded as valueless and thus dissociated from goodness. The important beginnings made before the Christian era in the direction of impersonal knowledge, physics, astronomy, mathematics, physiology, etc., were brought to an end by this indifference to the physical world (animate or inanimate) and its truths, and by this denial to man of the constructive exercise of his aggression.[1]

Not only, however, does the *dissociation* and exclusion of aggression from fusion and partnership with love lead to its discharge in extreme forms of destructiveness ; another aspect of the situation results specifically from the *denial* of it. Without aggression for means of subsistence, and without sexuality for race preservation, human life would cease to exist. It is objectively untrue to deny the necessity and decry the value of what is so essential to life. And it is equally false to deny or decry the necessity or value of man's pleasure in the functioning

[1] The changes to which I refer briefly here, in the social consciousness, the ideas, interests and contents of men's minds at different periods, and in their ways of regarding the world, are illustrated in a most illuminating fashion by the evidence of language in a book to which I am indebted for many new and valuable impressions: *The English Language* (particularly Chap. IX), by L. Pearsall Smith. Home University Library.

of his physical body and his sexual and aggressive instincts. Without sufficient instinctual satisfaction life itself becomes valueless to man; he is reduced to apathy and uselessness. A denial of the existence and value of these instincts in man is therefore an illusion, and is to that extent a false foundation upon which to build a way of life. All the efforts made to support and confirm it then only augment the self-deception in it. The attempt to apply it to reality, and to deal with reality on the basis of a denial, soon calls for active dissimulation and falsity to support it against the force of truth. For instance, smugness, cant, and hypocrisy—some of the forms of indirect and insidious aggression—then undermine and discredit the constructive aspect of the dissociation of aggression from love, i.e. the value of altruistic love. This gives rise to anxiety and doubt, or to cynicism; and so faith in goodness is in danger of being lost altogether.

At this point in history severe disillusionment, accompanied by extreme insecurity, depression and helplessness, might have manifested itself, had not a gradual reaction set in, which is now perhaps reaching a climax. (It is evidence of the highly constructive character of many aspects of the Christian religion that it has been able for some time to absorb and to survive much of this reaction.) The desire to preserve goodness and the need for greater honesty forced a way through. It took the direction of interest in the *external* world and of *a search for truth and goodness in material things*, a tendency that revived at the Renaissance when some of the pre-Christian interests were rediscovered. This released aggression from its bonds and freed it again for science and for the attack on nature ; it led to the appreciation of material reality,[1] as against the concern with the emotional life, and to greater understanding and use of the material world—and hence to greater prosperity. It seems, however, that we may now be nearing the point at which external goodness—prosperity and material gains—will have taken the place of internal goodness as our ideal. Prosperity, as we all know, is a great aid, though not actually a means, towards inner goodness; it is, however, not a substitute for it. And if material gain becomes the ideal, the inner life of man is by so much denied and may itself come into contempt. The effect of this reaction is that a considerable *dissociation and denial of the part played in life by our inner emotional needs* has now come about. Our need to love, as our strongest security against the anxiety of hate and destructiveness within, together with the problems of guilt which are inseparable from love, and the standards of conscience and morality that spring from our guilt, all suffer from neglect, are denied, and may starve in their turn though material prosperity increases.

Prosperity as an ideal is concrete and definite; we can test and prove our success in attaining it. The ideal of inner goodness sets a far harder goal. Our love is internal and undemonstrable to ourselves; greed and hate are strong in us and faith in our love is not easy to attain. It is easy to scoff at and stifle

[1] Science inevitably started life in the easiest field for its purposes, that of the facts of the physical external world, which are more readily ascertainable and calculable than those of the internal world of man's mind (psychical reality). The discovery of the psychoanalytic technique, however, has made this further task much more feasible.

love, impossible to count it like a bank balance; one may readily be deceived about it and mistake for it what is not really love. Self-deception and unwarranted self-satisfaction easily attend the search for inner goodness. And if the conscience and morality within us are not the representatives of our love, they become vehicles of our hate; if they are deluded, they dupe us in turn. They may then, for example, mislead us into the complacent search for badness, partly indeed as a defence against self-deception. But since we find evil more readily in others than in ourselves, this is no cure for self-deception. All these dangers and difficulties tend to turn us away from the problems of goodness within, for fear of disillusionment, and the helplessness and insecurity that then threaten us.

External satisfactions are being grasped, therefore, while the even more difficult struggle for inner riches and peace of mind has been left to look after itself. It is well known that matters of conscience have gone out of fashion and that morality nowadays has a provincial air. Our inner psychological struggles—between our love and our hate—are receiving but little aid from conscious attention and efforts. It is true that the great necessity within us to encourage and nurture love, to give and receive it, and to suppress, deflect and modify hate, is seeking new outlets externally in our lives; but as an inner problem in each one of us it is obtaining little direct support. In its search for genuine goodness and in its fear of being deceived, this age of ' realism ' may have overshot a mark; there is reality within us as well as without, the facts not only of our ruthlessness and greed but also of our need to love and to be loving, which we suppress and do not honestly avow. Some of the

needed support for honesty and goodness within—
which are part of internal emotional reality and the
source of stable emotional security—should be available in mental science before long.[1] The psychological situation is that our love impulses are being
discounted and suppressed, have not enough support
or outlet, and so cannot pull their weight in the
interaction of love and hate. Consequently the
vicious circle of aggression and disruption is increasing its momentum; the Western civilization which
owes so much to the power of love may even be
destroyed. I do not suggest that life itself is in danger
of extinction by the destructive forces in man, but
that at the moment, love with its power of unification
being at a discount and so hard pressed by aggression,
the civilized form of life seems to be in danger of
disintegration.

An artificial segregation and discussion of the hate
in emotional life, such as has been attempted here,
is, you must remember, entirely schematic, and is
no representation of life as a whole. I hope that
my presentation of it will not have proved depressing.
It is of great importance that this side of our lives
should be better understood. When we become able
to accept both the inevitability and the potential
value of these processes in ourselves, the archaic
element in our fear of them and reactions to them
diminishes and is controlled ; and we devise means

[1] In fact many churchmen and mystics, though not
the Church itself, seem to have struggled to find this
goal. The scientific understanding of man's emotional
life, which is being acquired through psycho-analysis,
opens a way for the individual towards the solution of
these problems and so towards peace of mind.

to allow these natural forces some outlet and to use them as fully as possible in constructive ways. This can come about only by understanding, which derives so much from tolerance, in other words, from imagination, sympathy and love.

LOVE, GUILT AND REPARATION

Melanie Klein

LOVE, GUILT AND REPARATION

THE two parts of this book discuss very different aspects of human emotions. The first, ' Hate, Greed and Aggression,' deals with the powerful impulses of hate which are a fundamental part of human nature. The second, in which I am attempting to give a picture of the equally powerful forces of love and the drive to reparation, is complementary to the first, for the apparent division implied in this mode of presentation does not actually exist in the human mind. In separating our topic in this way we cannot perhaps clearly convey the constant *interaction* of love and hate ; but the division of this vast subject was necessary, for only when consideration has been given to the part that destructive impulses play in the interaction of hate and love, is it possible to show the ways in which feelings of love and tendencies to reparation develop in connection with aggressive impulses and in spite of them.

Joan Riviere's chapter made it clear that these emotions first appear in the early relation of the child to his mother's breasts, and that they are experienced fundamentally in connection with the desired person. It is necessary to go back to the mental life of the baby in order to study the interaction of all the various forces which go to build up this most complex of all human emotions which we call love.

The Emotional Situation of the Baby

The baby's first object of love and hate—his mother—is both desired and hated with all the intensity and strength that is characteristic of the early urges of the baby. In the very beginning he loves his mother at the time that she is satisfying his needs for nourishment, alleviating his feelings of hunger, and giving him the sensual pleasure which he experiences when his mouth is stimulated by sucking at her breast. This gratification is an essential part of the child's sexuality, and is indeed its initial expression. But when the baby is hungry and his desires are not gratified, or when he is feeling bodily pain or discomfort, then the whole situation suddenly alters. Hatred and aggressive feelings are aroused and he becomes dominated by the impulses to destroy the very person who is the object of all his desires and who in his mind is linked up with everything he experiences—good and bad alike. In the baby hatred and aggressive feelings give rise, moreover, as Joan Riviere has shown in detail, to most painful states, such as choking, breathlessness and other sensations of the kind, which are felt to be destructive to his own body, thus aggression, unhappiness and fears are again increased.

The immediate and primary means by which relief is afforded to a baby from these painful states of hunger, hate, tension and fear is the satisfaction of his desires by his mother. The temporary feeling of security which is gained by receiving gratification greatly enhances the gratification itself ; and thus a feeling of security becomes an important component of the satisfaction whenever a person receives love. This applies to the baby as well as to the adult, to the more simple forms

of love and to its most elaborate manifestations.
Because our mother first satisfied all our self-
preservative needs and sensual desires and gave us
security, the part she plays in our minds is a lasting
one, although the various ways in which this
influence is effected and the forms it takes may not
be at all obvious in later life. For instance, a
woman may apparently have estranged herself
from her mother, yet still unconsciously seek some
of the features of her early relation to her in her
relation to her husband or to a man she loves. The
very important part which the father plays in the
child's emotional life also influences all later love
relations, and all other human associations. But
the baby's early relation to him, in so far as he is
felt as a gratifying, friendly and protective figure,
is partly modelled on the one to the mother.

The baby, to whom his mother is primarily only
an object which satisfies all his desires—a good
breast,[1] as it were—soon begins to respond to these

[1] In order to simplify my description of the very
complicated and unfamiliar phenomena that I present
in this lecture, I am throughout, in speaking of the
feeding situation of the baby, referring to breast-feeding
only. Much of what I am saying in connection with
breast-feeding and the inferences I am drawing apply
to bottle-feeding also, though with certain differences.
In this connection I will quote a passage from my
chapter on 'Weaning' in *On the Bringing Up of Children*,
by Five Psycho-Analysts (Kegan Paul, 1936) : ' The
bottle is a substitute for the mother's breast, for it
allows the baby to have the pleasure of sucking and
thus to establish to a certain degree the breast-mother
relationship in connection with the bottle given by the
mother or nurse. Experience shows that often children
who have not been breast-fed develop quite well.

gratifications and to her care by developing feelings
of love towards her as a person. But this first love
is already disturbed at its roots by destructive
impulses. Love and hate are struggling together in
the baby's mind ; and this struggle to a certain
extent persists throughout life and is liable to
become a source of danger in human relationships.

The baby's impulses and feelings are accompanied
by a kind of mental activity which I take to be the
most primitive one : that is phantasy-building,
or more colloquially, imaginative thinking. For instance, the baby who feels a craving for his mother's
breast when it is not there may imagine it to be
there, i.e. he may imagine the satisfaction which he
derives from it. Such primitive phantasying is the
earliest form of the capacity which later develops
into the more elaborate workings of the imagination.

The early phantasies which go along with the
baby's feelings are of various kinds. In the one
just mentioned he imagines the gratification which

Still, in psycho-analysis one will always discover in
such people a deep longing for the breast which has
never been fulfilled, and though the breast-mother
relationship has been established to a certain degree, it
makes all the difference to the psychic development that
the earliest and fundamental gratification has been
obtained from a substitute, instead of from the real
thing which was desired. One may say that although
children can develop well without being breast-fed,
the development would have been different and better
in one way or another had they had a successful breast-
feeding. On the other hand, I infer from my experience
that children whose development goes wrong, even
though they have been breast-fed, would have been
more ill without it.'

he lacks. Pleasant phantasies, however, also accompany actual satisfaction ; and destructive phantasies go along with frustration and the feelings of hatred which this arouses. When a baby feels frustrated at the breast, in his phantasies he attacks this breast ; but if he is being gratified by the breast, he loves it and has phantasies of a pleasant kind in relation to it. In his aggressive phantasies he wishes to bite up and to tear up his mother and her breasts, and to destroy her also in other ways.

A most important feature of these destructive phantasies, which are tantamount to death-wishes, is that the baby feels that what he desires in his phantasies has really taken place ; that is to say he feels that he *has really destroyed* the object of his destructive impulses, and is going on destroying it : this has extremely important consequences for the development of his mind. The baby finds support against these fears in omnipotent phantasies of a restoring kind : that too has extremely important consequences for his development. If the baby has, in his aggressive phantasies, injured his mother by biting and tearing her up, he may soon build up phantasies that he is putting the bits together again and repairing her.[1] This, however, does not quite do away with his fears of having destroyed the object which, as we know, is the one whom he loves and needs most, and on whom he is

[1] The psycho-analysis of small children, which enabled me to draw conclusions also as to the workings of the mind at an earlier stage, has convinced me that such phantasies are already active in babies. Psychoanalysis of adults has shown me that the effects of this early phantasy-life are lasting, and profoundly influence the unconscious mind of the grown-up person.

entirely dependent. In my view, these basic conflicts profoundly influence the course and the force of
the emotional lives of grown-up individuals.

Unconscious Sense of Guilt

We all know that if we detect in ourselves impulses
of hate towards a person we love, we feel concerned
or guilty. As Coleridge puts it :

> . . . to be wroth with one we love,
> Doth work like madness in the brain.

We tend very much to keep these feelings of guilt in
the background, because of their painfulness. They
express themselves, however, in many disguised
ways, and are a source of disturbance in our personal relations. For instance, some people readily
experience distress through lack of appreciation,
even from persons who mean but little to them ;
the reason is that in their' unconscious minds they
feel unworthy of man's regard, and a cold reception
confirms their suspicion of this unworthiness. Others
are dissatisfied with themselves (not on objective
grounds) in the most various ways, for example,
in connection with their appearance, their work,
or their abilities in general. Some of these manifestations are quite commonly recognized and have been
popularly termed an ' inferiority complex.'
Psycho-analytic findings show that feelings of this
kind are more deeply rooted than is usually supposed
and are always connected with unconscious feelings
of guilt. The reason why some people have so
strong a need for general praise and approval lies
in their need for evidence that they are lovable,
worthy of love. This feeling arises from the unconscious fear of being incapable of loving others

sufficiently or truly, and particularly of not being able to master aggressive impulses towards others : they dread being a danger to the loved one.

Love and Conflicts in Relation to the Parents

The struggle between love and hate, with all the conflicts to which it gives rise, sets in, as I have tried to show, in early infancy, and is active all through life. It begins with the child's relationship to both parents. In the relation of the suckling to his mother, sensual feelings are already present and express themselves in the pleasurable mouth sensations connected with the sucking process. Soon genital feelings come to the fore and the craving for the mother's nipples diminishes. It does not altogether vanish, however, but remains active in the unconscious and partly also in the conscious mind. Now in the case of the little girl the concern with the nipple passes over to an interest, which is for the most part unconscious, in the father's genital, and this becomes the object of her libidinal wishes and phantasies. As development proceeds, the little girl desires her father more than her mother, and has conscious and unconscious phantasies of taking her mother's place, winning her father for herself and becoming his wife. She is also very jealous of the children her mother possesses, and wishes her father to give her babies of her own. These feelings, wishes and phantasies go along with rivalry, aggression and hatred against her mother, and are added to the grievances which she felt against her because of the earliest frustrations at the breast. Nevertheless, sexual phantasies and desires towards her mother do remain active in the little girl's

mind. Under the influence of these she wants to
take her father's place in connection with her
mother, and in certain cases these desires and
phantasies may develop more strongly even than
those towards the father. Thus besides the love to
both of them there are also feelings of rivalry to
both, and this mixture of feelings is carried further
in her relation to brothers and sisters. The desires
and phantasies in connection with mother and
sisters are the basis for direct homosexual relationships in later life, as well as for homosexual feelings
which express themselves indirectly in friendship
and affection between women. In the ordinary
course of events these homosexual desires recede
into the background, become deflected and sublimated, and the attraction towards the other sex
predominates.

A corresponding development takes place in the
small boy, who soon experiences genital desires
towards his mother and feelings of hatred against
his father as a rival. But in him, too, genital desires
towards his father develop, and this is the root of
homosexuality in men. These situations give rise
to many conflicts—for the little girl, although she
hates her mother, also loves her ; and the little boy
loves his father and would spare him the danger
arising from his—the boy's—aggressive impulses.
Moreover, the main object of all sexual desires—
in the girl, the father, in the boy, the mother—also
rouses hate and revenge, because these desires are
disappointed.

The child is also intensely jealous of brothers and
sisters, in so far as they are rivals for the parents'
love. He also loves them, however, and thus again
in this connection strong conflicts between aggressive

impulses and feelings of love are aroused. This leads to feelings of guilt and again to wishes to make good : a mixture of feelings which has an important bearing not only on our relations with brothers and sisters but, since relations to people in general are modelled on the same pattern, also on our social attitude and on feelings of love and guilt and the wish to make good in later life.

Love, Guilt and Reparation

I said before that feelings of love and gratitude arise directly and spontaneously in the baby in response to the love and care of his mother. The power of love—which is the manifestation of the forces which tend to preserve life—is there in the baby as well as the destructive impulses, and finds its first fundamental expression in the baby's attachment to his mother's breast, which develops into love for her as a person. My psycho-analytic work has convinced me that when in the baby's mind the conflicts between love and hate arise, and the fears of losing the loved one become active, a very important step is made in development. These feelings of guilt and distress now enter as a new element into the emotion of love. They become an inherent part of love, and influence it profoundly both in quality and quantity.

Even in the small child one can observe a concern for the loved one which is not, as one might think, merely a sign of dependence upon a friendly and helpful person. Side by side with the destructive impulses in the unconscious mind both of the child and of the adult, there exists a profound urge to make sacrifices, in order to help and to put right loved people who in phantasy have been harmed or destroyed. In the depths of the mind, the urge to make people happy is linked up with a strong feeling of responsibility and concern for them, which manifests itself in genuine sympathy with other people and in the ability to understand them, as they are and as they feel.

Identification and Making Reparation

To be genuinely considerate implies that we can put ourselves in the place of other people : we ' identify ' ourselves with them. Now. this capacity for identification with another person is a most important element in human relationships in general, and is also a condition for real and strong feelings of love. We are only able to disregard or to some extent sacrifice our own feelings and desires, and thus for a time to put the other person's interests and emotions first, if we have the capacity to identify ourselves with the loved person. Since in being identified with other people we share, as it were, the help or satisfaction afforded to them by ourselves, we regain in one way what we have sacrificed in another.[1]   Ultimately,   in   making

---

[1] As I said at the beginning there is a constant interaction of love and hate in all of us. My topic, however, is concerned with the ways in which feelings of love develop and become strengthened and stabilized. Since I am not entering much into questions of aggression I must make clear that it is also active, even in people whose capacity for love is strongly developed. Generally speaking, in such people both aggression and hatred (the latter diminished and to some degree counterbalanced by the capacity for love) is used very greatly in constructive ways (' sublimated,' as it has been termed). There is actually no productive activity

sacrifices for somebody we love and in identifying ourselves with the loved person, we play the part of a good parent, and behave towards this person as we felt at times the parents did to us—or as we wanted them to do. At the same time, we also play the part of the good child towards his parents, which we wished to do in the past and are now acting out in the present. Thus, by reversing a situation, namely in acting towards another person as a good parent, in phantasy we re-create and enjoy the wished-for love and goodness of our parents. But to act as good parents towards other people may also be a way of dealing with the frustrations and sufferings of the past. Our grievances against our parents for having frustrated us, together with the feelings of hate and revenge to which these have given rise in us, and again, the feelings of guilt and despair arising out of this hate and revenge because

into which some aggression does not enter in one way or another. Take, for instance, the housewife's occupation : cleaning and so on certainly bear witness to her desire to make things pleasant for others and for herself, and as such is a manifestation of love for other people and for the things she cares for. But at the same time she also gives expression to her aggression in destroying the enemy, dirt, which in her unconscious mind has come to stand for ' bad ' things. The original hatred and aggression derived from the earliest sources may break through in women whose cleanliness becomes obsessional. We all know the type of women who make life miserable for the family by continuously ' tidying up ' ; there the hatred is actually turned against the people she loves and cares for. To hate people and things which are felt to be worthy of hate— be they people we dislike or principles (political, artistic, religious or moral) with which we disagree, is a general we have injured the parents whom at the same time we loved—all these, in phantasy, we may undo in retrospect (taking away some of the grounds for hatred), by playing at the same time the parts of loving parents and loving children. At the same time, in our unconscious phantasy we make good the injuries which we did in phantasy, and for which we still unconsciously feel very guilty. This *making reparation* is, in my view, a fundamental element in love and in all human relationships; I shall therefore refer to it frequently in what follows.

way of giving vent, in a manner which is felt to be permissible and can actually be quite constructive, to our feelings of hatred, aggression, scorn and contempt, if it does not go to extremes. These emotions, though made use of in adult ways, are at bottom the ones we experienced in childhood when we hated the people whom at the same time we also loved—our parents. Even then we attempted to keep our love towards our parents, and to turn the hatred on to other people and things, a process which is more successful when we have developed and stabilized our capacity for love and also extended our range of interests, affections and hatreds in adult life. To give a few more examples: the work of lawyers, politicians and critics involves combating opponents, but in ways which are felt to be allowable and useful; and here again the foregoing conclusions would apply. One of the many ways in which aggression can be expressed legitimately and even laudably is in games, in which the opponent is temporarily—and this fact of its being temporary also helps to diminish the sense of guilt—attacked with feelings that again derive from early emotional situations. There are thus many ways—sublimated and direct—in which aggression and hatreds find expression in people who are at the same time very kind-hearted and capable of love.

A Happy Love Relationship

Bearing in mind what I have said about the origins of love, let us now consider some particular relationships of adults, taking first, as an example, a satisfactory and stable love relationship between a man and a woman, as it may be found in a happy marriage. This implies a deep attachment, a capacity for mutual sacrifice, a sharing—in grief as well as in pleasure, in interests as well as in sexual enjoyment. A relationship of this nature affords the widest scope for the most varied manifestations of love.[1] If the woman has a maternal attitude towards the man, she satisfies (as far as can be) his earliest wishes for the gratifications he desired from his own mother. In the past, these wishes have never been quite satisfied, and have never been quite given up. The man has now, as it were, this mother for his own, with relatively little feeling of guilt. (I shall go into the reason for this in more detail later.) If the woman has a richly developed emotional life, besides possessing these maternal feelings, she will also have kept something of the child's attitude towards her father, and some of the features of this old relationship will enter into her relation to her husband ; for instance, she will trust and admire

[1] In considering adult emotions and relationships I shall throughout this paper deal mainly with the bearing the child's early impulses and unconscious feelings and phantasies have upon the later manifestations of love. I am aware that this necessarily leads to a somewhat one-sided and schematic presentation, for in this way I cannot do justice to the multiple factors that in the life-long interaction between influences coming from the outer world and the individual's inner forces work together to build up an adult relationship.

her husband, and he will be a protective and helpful figure to her as her father was. These feelings will be a foundation for a relation in which the woman's desires and needs as a grown-up person can find full satisfaction. Again, this attitude of his wife's gives the man the opportunity to be protective and helpful to her in various ways—that is, in his unconscious mind, to play the part of a good husband to his mother.

If the woman is capable of strong feelings of love both towards her husband and towards her children, one can infer that she has most probably had a good relationship in childhood to both parents, and to her brothers and sisters ; that is to say, that she has been able to deal satisfactorily with her early feelings of hate and revenge against them. I have mentioned before the importance of the little girl's unconscious wish to receive a baby from her father, and of the sexual desires towards him which are connected with this wish. The father's frustration of her genital desires gives rise to intense aggressive phantasies in the child, which have an important bearing upon the capacity for sexual gratification in adult life. Sexual phantasies in the little girl thus become connected with hatred which is specifically directed against her father's penis, because she feels that it denies her the gratification which it affords to her mother. In her jealousy and hatred she wishes it to be a dangerous and evil thing—one which could not gratify her mother either—and the penis thus, in her phantasy, acquires destructive qualities. Because of these unconscious wishes, which focus on her parents' sexual gratifications, in some of her phantasies sexual organs and sexual gratification take on a bad and dangerous character. These aggressive phantasies are again followed in the child's mind by wishes to make good—more specifically, by phantasies of healing the father's genital which, in her mind, she has injured or made bad. The phantasies of a curative nature are also connected with sexual feelings and desires. All these unconscious phantasies influence greatly the woman's feelings towards her husband. If he loves her and also gratifies her sexually, her unconscious sadistic phantasies will lose in strength. But since these are not entirely put out of action (though in a woman who is fairly normal, they are not present in a degree that inhibits the tendency to blend with more positive or friendly erotic impulses), they lead to a stimulation of phantasies of a restoring nature ; thus once more the drive to make reparation is brought into action. Sexual gratification affords her not only pleasure, but reassurance and support against the fears and feelings of guilt which were the result of her early sadistic wishes. This reassurance enhances sexual gratification and gives rise in the woman to feelings of gratitude, tenderness and increased love. Just because there is somewhere in the depths of her mind a feeling that her genital is dangerous and could injure her husband's genital— which is a derivative of her aggressive phantasies towards her father—one part of the satisfaction she obtains comes from the fact that she is capable of giving her husband pleasure and happiness, and that her genital thus proves to be good.

Because the little girl had phantasies of her father's genital being dangerous, these still have a certain influence upon the woman's unconscious mind. But if she has a happy and sexually gratifying relation with her husband, his genital is felt to be good, and thus her fears of the bad genital are disproved. The sexual gratification thus works as a double reassurance : of her own goodness and of her husband's, and the feeling of security gained in this way adds to the actual sexual enjoyment. The circle of reassurance thus provided is still wider. The woman's early jealousy and hatred of her mother as a rival for her father's love has played an important part in her aggressive phantasies. The mutual happiness provided both by sexual gratification and by a happy and loving relation to her husband will also be felt partly as an indication that her sadistic wishes against her mother have not taken effect, or that reparation has succeeded.

The emotional attitude and the sexuality of a man in his relation to his wife are of course also influenced by his past. The frustration by his mother of his genital desires in his childhood aroused phantasies in which his penis became an instrument which could give pain and cause injury to her. At the same time jealousy and hatred of his father as a rival for his mother's love set going phantasies of a sadistic nature against his father also. In the sexual relation to his love-partner the man's early aggressive phantasies, which led to a fear of his penis being destructive, come into play to some extent, and by a transmutation similar in kind to that described for the woman, the sadistic impulse, when it is in manageable quantity, stimulates phantasies of reparation. The penis is then felt to be a good and curative organ, which shall afford the woman pleasure, cure her injured genital and create babies in her. A happy and sexually gratifying relationship with the woman affords him proofs of the goodness of his penis, and also unconsciously gives him the feeling that his wishes to restore her have succeeded. This not only increases his sexual pleasure and his love and tenderness for the woman, but here again it leads to feelings of gratitude and security. In addition, these feelings are apt to increase his creative powers in other ways and to influence his capacity for work and for other activities. If his wife can share in his interests (as well as in love and in sexual satisfaction), she affords him proofs of the value of his work. In these various ways his early wish to be capable of doing what his father did for his mother, sexually and otherwise, and to receive from her what his father received, can be fulfilled in his relation to his wife. His happy relation to her has also the effect of diminishing his aggression against his father, which was greatly stimulated by his being unable to have his mother as a wife, and this may reassure him that his long-standing sadistic tendencies against his father have not been effective. Since grievances and hatred against his father have influenced his feelings towards men who have come to stand for his father, and grievances against his mother have affected his relation to women who stand for her, a satisfactory love relationship alters his outlook on life and his attitude to people and activities in general. To possess his wife's love and appreciation gives him a feeling of being fully grown-up and thus of being equal to his father. The hostile and aggressive rivalry with him diminishes and gives way to a more friendly competition with his father—or rather with admired father-figures—in productive functions and achievements, and this is very likely to enhance or increase his productivity.

Similarly, when a woman in a happy love

relationship with a man unconsciously feels that she can take, as it were, the place that her mother took with *her* husband, and now gains satisfactions that her mother enjoyed and that she, as a child, was denied—then she is able to feel equal to her mother, to enjoy the same happiness, rights and privileges as her mother did, but without injuring and robbing her. The effects upon her attitude and the development of her personality are analogous to the changes which take place in the man when he finds himself, in a happy married life, equal to his father.

Thus in both partners a relationship of mutual sexual gratification and love will be felt as a happy re-creation of their early family lives. Many wishes and phantasies can never be satisfied in childhood,[1]

[1] In the case of the boy, for example, the child wishes to have his mother to himself the whole twenty-four hours of the day, to have sexual intercourse with her, to give her babies, to kill his father because he is jealous of him, to deprive his brothers and sisters of everything they have, and turn them out too if they get in his way. It is obvious that if these impracticable wishes were fulfilled they would cause him the deepest feelings of guilt. Even the realization of much less far-reaching destructive desires is apt to arouse deep conflicts. For instance many a child will feel guilty if he becomes his mother's favourite, because his father and brothers and sisters will be correspondingly neglected. This is what I mean by saying there are simultaneously contradictory wishes in the unconscious mind. The child's desires are unlimited and so are his destructive impulses in connection with these desires, but at the same time he also has—unconsciously and consciously—opposite tendencies; he also wishes to give them love and make reparation. He himself actually wants to be restrained by the adults around him in his aggression and selfishness, because if these are

not only because they are impracticable, but also because there are simultaneously contradictory wishes in the unconscious mind. It seems a paradoxical fact that, in a way, fulfilment of many infantile wishes is possible only when the individual has grown up. In the happy relationship of grown-up people the early wish to have one's mother or father all to oneself is still unconsciously active. Of course, reality does not allow one to be one's mother's husband or one's father's wife ; and had it been possible, feelings of guilt towards others would have interfered with the gratification. But only if one has been able to develop such relationships with the parents in unconscious phantasy, and has been able

given free rein he is caused suffering by the pain of remorse and unworthiness; and in fact he relies on obtaining this help from grown-ups, like any other help he needs. Consequently it is psychologically quite inadequate to attempt to solve children's difficulties by not frustrating them at all. Naturally, frustration which is in reality unnecessary or arbitrary and shows nothing but lack of love and understanding is very detrimental. It is important to realize that the child's development depends on, and to a large extent is formed by, his capacity to find the way to bear inevitable and necessary frustrations and the conflicts of love and hate which are in part caused by them : that is, to find his way between his hate which is increased by frustrations, and his love and wish for reparation which bring in their train the sufferings of remorse. The way the child adapts himself to these problems in his mind forms the foundation for all his later social relationships, his adult capacity for love and cultural development. He can be immensely helped in childhood by the love and understanding of those around him, but these deep problems can neither be solved for him nor abolished.

to overcome to some extent one's feelings of guilt
connected with these phantasies, and gradually to
detach oneself from as well as remaining attached
to the parents, is one capable of transferring these
wishes to other people, who then stand for desired
objects of the past, though they are not identical
with them. That is to say, only if the individual has
grown up in the real sense of the word can his
infantile phantasies be fulfilled in the adult state.
What is more, guilt due to these infantile wishes then
becomes relieved, just because a situation phantasied
in childhood has now become real in a permissible
way, and in a way which proves that the injuries of
various kinds, which in phantasy were connected
with this situation, have not actually been inflicted.

A happy adult relationship, such as I have described, can thus, as I said before, mean a re-
creation of the early family situation, and this will
be the more complete, and therefore the whole
circle of reassurance and security will be wider
still, through the relation of the man and woman
to their children. This brings us to the subject of
parenthood.

Parenthood : On Being a Mother

We will consider first a really loving relationship of
a mother to her baby, as it develops if the woman has
attained a fully maternal personality. There are
many threads which link the relationship of the
mother to her child with that of her own relation
to her mother in babyhood. A very strong conscious
and unconscious wish for babies exists in small
children. In the little girl's unconscious phantasies,
her mother's body is full of babies. These she
imagines have been put into her by her father's

penis, which is to her the symbol of all creativeness, power and goodness. This predominant attitude of admiration towards her father and his sexual organs as creative and life-giving goes along with the little girl's intense desire to possess children of her own and to have babies inside her, as the most precious possession.

It is an everyday observation that little girls play with dolls as if these were their babies. But a child will often display a passionate devotion to the doll, for it has become to her a live and real baby, a companion, a friend, which forms part of her life. She not only carries it about with her, but constantly has it in her mind, starts the day with it and gives it up unwillingly if she is made to do something else. These wishes experienced in childhood persist into womanhood and contribute greatly to the strength of the love that a pregnant woman feels for the child growing inside her, and then for the baby to which she has given birth. The gratification of at last having it relieves the pain of the frustration experienced in childhood when she wanted a baby from her father and could not have it. This long-postponed fulfilment of an all-important wish tends to make her less aggressive and to increase her capacity for loving her child. Furthermore, the child's helplessness and its great need for its mother's care call for more love than can be given to any other person, and thus all the mother's loving and constructive tendencies now have scope. Some mothers, as we know, exploit this relationship for the gratification of their own desires, i.e. their possessiveness and the satisfaction of having somebody dependent upon them. Such women want their children to cling to them, and

they hate them to grow up and to acquire individu-
alities of their own. With others, the child's helplessness calls out all the strong wishes to make
reparation, which are derived from various sources
and which can now be related to this most wished-
for baby, who is the fulfilment of her early longings.
Gratitude towards the child who affords his mother
the enjoyment of being able to love him enhances
these feelings, and may lead to an attitude where the
mother's first concern will be for the baby's good,
and her own gratification will become bound up
with his welfare.

The nature of the relations of the mother to her
children alters, of course, as they grow up. Her
attitude to her older children will be more or less
influenced by her attitude to her brothers and
sisters, cousins, etc., in the past. Certain difficulties
in these past relationships may easily interfere with
her feelings to her own child, especially if it develops
reactions and traits which tend to stir these difficulties in her. Her jealousy and rivalry towards
her brothers and sisters gave rise to death-wishes
and aggressive phantasies, in which in her mind
she injured or destroyed them. If her sense of guilt
and the conflicts derived from these phantasies
are not too strong, then the possibility of making
reparation can have more scope and her maternal
feelings can come more fully into play.

One element in this maternal attitude seems to be
that the mother is capable of putting herself in the
child's place and of looking at the situation from
his point of view. Her being able to do so with love
and sympathy is closely bound up, as we have seen,
with feelings of guilt and the drive to reparation.
If, however, the sense of guilt is over-strong, this

identification may lead to an entirely self-sacrificing attitude which is very much to the child's disadvantage. It is well known that a child who has been brought up by a mother who showers love on him and expects nothing in return often becomes a selfish person. Lack of capacity for love and consideration in a child is, to a certain extent, a cover for over-strong feelings of guilt. A mother's over-indulgence tends to increase feelings of quiet, and moreover does not allow enough scope for the child's own tendencies to make reparation, to make sacrifices sometimes, and to develop true consideration for others.[1]

If, however, the mother is not too closely wrapped up in the child's feelings and is not too much identified with him, she is able to use her wisdom in guiding the child in the most helpful way. She will then get full satisfaction from the possibility of furthering the child's development—a satisfaction which is again enhanced by phantasies of doing for her child what her own mother did for her, or what she wished her mother to do. In achieving this, she also repays her mother and makes good the injuries done, in phantasy, to her mother's children, and this again lessens her feelings of guilt.

A mother's capacity to love and to understand her children will be especially tested when they come to the stage of adolescence. At this period,

[1] A similar detrimental effect (though this comes about in a different way) is produced by harshness or lack of love on the part of parents.—This touches on the important problem of how the environment influences the child's emotional development in a favourable or unfavourable way. This, however, is beyond the scope of the present paper.

children normally tend to turn away from their parents and to free themselves to a certain degree from their old attachments to them. The children's striving to find their way towards new objects of love creates situations which are apt to be very painful for parents. If the mother has strong maternal feelings, she can remain unshaken in her love, can be patient and understanding, give help and advice where this is necessary, and yet allow the children to work out their problems for themselves—and she may be able to do all this without asking much for herself. This is only possible, however, if her capacity for love has developed in such a way that she can make a strong identification both with her child, and with a wise mother of her own whom she keeps in her mind.

The mother's relations to her children will again alter in character and her love may manifest itself in different ways when her children are grown up, have made lives of their own and freed themselves from old ties. The mother may now find that she has not a large part to play in their lives. But she may find some satisfaction in keeping her love prepared for them whenever it is needed. She thus feels unconsciously that she affords them security, and is forever the mother of the early days, whose breast gave them full gratification and who satisfied their needs and their desires. In this situation, the mother has identified herself fully with her own helpful mother, whose protective influence has never ceased to function in her mind. At the same time she is also identified with her own children : she is, in her phantasy, as it were, again a child, and shares with her children the possession of a good and helpful mother. The unconscious minds of the children very often correspond to the mother's unconscious mind, and whether or not they make much use of this store of love prepared for them, they often gain great inner support and comfort through the knowledge that this love exists.

Parenthood : On Being a Father

Although his children do not on the whole mean so much to the man as to the woman, they do play an important part in his life, especially if he and his wife are in harmony. To go back to deeper sources of this relationship, I have already referred to the gratification which a man derives from giving a baby to his wife, in so far as this means making up for his sadistic wishes towards his mother and making restoration to her. This increases the actual satisfaction of creating a baby and of fulfilling his wife's wishes. An additional source of pleasure is the gratification of his feminine wishes by his sharing the maternal pleasure of his wife. As a small boy he had strong desires to bear children as his mother did, and these desires increased his tendencies to rob her of her children. As a man, he can *give* children to his wife, can see her happy with them, and is then able, without feeling guilty, to identify himself with her in her bearing and suckling of their children, and again in her relation to the older children.

There are many satisfactions, however, which he derives from being able to be a *good father* to his children. All his protective feelings, which have been stimulated by feelings of guilt in connection with the early family life when he was a child, find full expression. Again, there is the identification with the good father—either with his actual father or with his ideal of a father. Another element in his relationship with his children is his strong identification with them, for he shares in his mind their enjoyments ; and, moreover, in helping them in their difficulties and promoting their development he is renewing his own childhood in a more satisfactory way.

Much of what I have said about the mother's relation to her children in different stages of their development applies also to the father's. He plays a different part from that of the mother, but their attitudes complement each other ; and if (as is assumed in this whole discussion) their married life is based upon love and understanding, the husband also enjoys his wife's relation with their children, whilst she takes pleasure in his understanding and helping them.

Difficulties in Family Relationships

A fully harmonious family life such as that implied in my description is, as we know, not an everyday occurrence. It depends upon a happy coincidence of circumstances and psychological factors, first of all, upon a well-developed faculty for love in both partners. Difficulties of all kinds may occur, both in the relation between husband and wife and in their relations to the children, and I will give a few examples of these.

The individuality of the child may not correspond to what the parents wished it to be. Either partner may unconsciously want the child to be like a brother or a sister of the past ; and this wish obviously cannot be satisfied in both parents—and may not be fulfilled even in one. Again, if there has been strong rivalry and jealousy in relation to brothers and sisters in either or both partners, this may be repeated in connection with the achievements and the development of their own children. Another situation of difficulty arises when the parents are over-ambitious and wish, by means of the achievements of their children, to gain reassurances for themselves and to lessen their own fears. Then, again, some mothers are not able to love and to enjoy the possession of their children because they feel too guilty of taking, in phantasy, their own mother's place. A woman of this type may not be able to tend her children herself, but has to leave them to the care of nurses or other people—who in her unconscious mind stand for her own mother, to whom she is thus returning the children whom she wished to take away from her. This fear of loving the child, which of course disturbs the relationship with the child, may occur in men as well as in women, and will probably affect the mutual relations of husband and wife.

I have said that feelings of guilt and the drive to make reparation are intimately bound up with the emotion of love. If, however, the early conflict between love and hate has not been satisfactorily dealt with, or if guilt is too strong, this may lead to a turning away from loved people or even to a rejection of them. In the last analysis it is the fear that the loved person—to begin with, the mother—may die because of the injuries inflicted upon her in phantasy, which makes it unbearable to be dependent upon this person. We can observe the satisfaction small children gain from their early achievements, and from everything which increases their independence. There are many obvious reasons for this, but a deep and important one is, in my experience, that the child is driven towards weakening his attachment to the all-important person, his mother. She originally kept his life going, supplied all his needs, protected him and gave him security; she is therefore felt as the source of all goodness and of life, in unconscious phantasy she becomes an inseparable part of oneself; her death would therefore imply one's own death. Where these feelings and phantasies are very strong, the attachment to loved people may become an overwhelming burden.

Many people find their way out of these difficulties by lessening their capacity for love, *denying* or suppressing it, and by avoiding strong emotions altogether. Others have found an escape from the dangers of love by having displaced it predominantly from people to something else but people. The displacement of love to things and interests (which I discuss in connection with the explorer and the man struggling with the hardships of nature) is part of normal growth. But with some people this displacement to objects other than human has become their main mode of dealing with, or rather escaping from, conflicts. We all know the type of animal lover, passionate collector, scientist, artist, and so on, who is capable of a great love, and often self-sacrifice, for the objects of his devotion or his chosen work, but has little interest and love to spare for his fellow-men.

A quite different development takes place in people who become entirely dependent upon those to whom they are strongly attached. With them, the unconscious fear that the loved one will die leads to over-dependence. Greed, which is increased by fears of the kind, is one element in such an attitude, and is expressed in making as much use as possible of the person on whom one is dependent.

Another constituent in this attitude of over-dependence is the shirking of responsibility : the other person is made responsible for one's actions, and sometimes even for one's opinions and thoughts. (This is one of the reasons why people accept without criticism the views of a leader and act with blind obedience to his commands.) With people who are so over-dependent, love is very much needed as a support against the sense of guilt and fears of various kinds. The loved person, by signs of affection, must prove to them over and over again that they are not bad, not aggressive, and that their destructive impulses have not taken effect.

These over-strong ties are especially disturbing in the relation of a mother to her child. As I have pointed out before, the attitude of a mother to her child has much in common with her feelings as a child towards her own mother. We know already that this early relationship is characterized by the conflicts between love and hate. Unconscious death-wishes which the child bears towards her mother are carried over to her own child when she becomes a mother. These feelings are increased by the conflicting emotions in childhood towards brothers and sisters. If as the result of unsolved conflict in the past the mother feels too guilty in relation to her own child, she may need its love so intensely that she uses various devices to tie it closely to herself and to make it dependent upon her ; or again, she may devote herself too much to the child, making him the centre of her whole life.

Let us consider now, though only from one basic aspect, a very different mental attitude—infidelity. The manifold forms and manifestations of infidelity (being the outcome of the most varied ways of development and expressing in some people mainly love, in others mainly hatred, with all degrees in between) have one phenomenon in common: the repeated turning away from a (loved) person, which partly springs from the fear of dependance. I have found that the typical Don Juan in the depths of his mind is haunted by the dread of the death of loved people, and that this fear would break through and express itself in feelings of depression and in great mental sufferings if he had not developed this particular defence—his infidelity—against them. By means of this he is proving to himself over and over again that his *one* greatly loved object (originally his mother, whose death he dreaded because he felt his love for her to be greedy and destructive), is not after all indispensable since he can always find another woman to whom he has passionate but shallow feelings. In contrast to those people whom a great dread of the death of the loved person drives to rejecting her or to stifling and denying love, he is, for various reasons, incapable of doing so. But through his attitude towards women an unconscious compromise finds expression. By deserting and rejecting some women he unconsciously turns away from his mother, saves her from his dangerous desires and frees himself from his painful dependence on her, and by turning to other women and giving them pleasure and love he is in his unconscious mind retaining the loved mother or re-creating her.

In reality he is driven from one person to another, since the other person soon comes to stand again for his mother. His original love object is thus replaced by a succession of different ones. In unconscious phantasy he is re-creating or healing his mother by means of sexual gratifications (which he actually gives to other women), for only in one aspect is his sexuality felt to be dangerous; in another aspect it is felt to be curative and to make her happy. This twofold attitude is part of the unconscious compromise which resulted in his infidelity and is one condition for his particular way of development.

This leads me to another type of difficulty in love relationships. A man may restrict his affectionate, tender and protective feelings to one woman, who may be his wife, but he is unable to get sexual enjoyment in this relationship, and has either to repress his sexual desires or to turn them towards some other woman. Fears of the destructive nature of his sexuality, fears of his father as a rival and feelings of guilt in this connection are deep reasons for such a separation of feelings of a tender kind from specifically sexual ones. The loved and highly valued woman, who stands for his mother, has to be saved from his sexuality, which in phantasy is felt to be dangerous.

Choice of Love-Partner

Psycho-analysis shows that there are deep unconscious motives which contribute to the choice of a love-partner, and make two particular people sexually attractive and satisfactory to each other. The feelings of a man towards a woman are always influenced by his early attachment to his mother. But here again this will be more or less unconscious, and may be very much disguised in its manifestations. A man may choose as a love-partner a woman who has some characteristics of an entirely opposite kind to those of his mother—perhaps the loved woman's appearance is quite different, but

her voice or some characteristics of her personality
are in accordance with his early impressions of his
mother and have a special attraction for him. Or
again, just because he wanted to get away from too
strong an attachment to his mother, he may choose
a love-partner who is in absolute contrast to her.

Very often, as development proceeds, a sister or a
cousin takes the mother's place in the boy's sexual
phantasies and feelings of love. It is obvious that
an attitude based on such feelings will differ from
that of a man who seeks mainly maternal traits in a
woman ; although a man whose choice is influenced
by his feelings for a sister may also seek some traits
of a maternal kind in his love-partner. A great
variety of possibilities is created by the early influence of various people in the child's environment :
a nurse, an aunt, a grandmother, may play an important part in this respect. Of course, in considering
the bearing early relationships have upon the later
choice, we must not forget that it is the impression
of the loved person that the child had at the time,
and the phantasies he connected with her then,
which he wishes to rediscover in his later love
relationship. Furthermore, the unconscious mind
does associate things on grounds other than those
the conscious mind is aware of. Completely for-
gotten—repressed—impressions of various kinds for
this reason contribute to make one person more
attractive, sexually and otherwise, than another to
the individual concerned.

Similar factors are at work in the woman's
choice. Her impressions of her father, her feelings
towards him—admiration, trust, and so on—may
play a predominant part in her choosing of a love
companion. But her early love to her father may

have been shaken. Perhaps she soon turned away from him because of over-strong conflicts, or because he disappointed her too much, and a brother, a cousin or a playmate, let us say, may have become a very important person to her; she may have had sexual desires and phantasies as well as maternal feelings towards him. She would then seek a lover or husband agreeing with this image of a brother rather than one who had qualities of a more fatherly kind. In a successful love relationship, the unconscious minds of the love-partners correspond. Taking the case of the woman who has mainly maternal feelings and is seeking a partner of a brotherly nature, then the man's phantasies and desires would correspond if he is looking for a predominantly maternal woman. If the woman is strongly tied to her father, then she unconsciously chooses a man who needs a woman to whom he can play the part of a good father.

Although love-relationships in adult life are founded upon early emotional situations in connection with parents, brothers and sisters, the new relationships are not necessarily mere repetitions of early family situations. Unconscious memories, feelings and phantasies enter into the new love-relationship or friendship in quite disguised ways. But besides early influences there are many other factors at work in the complicated processes that build up a love-relationship or a friendship. Normal adult relationships always contain fresh elements which are derived from the new situation—from circumstances and the personalities of the people we come in contact with, and from their response to our emotional needs and practical interests as grown-up people.

Achieving Independence

So far I have spoken mainly of intimate relationships between people. We now come to the more general manifestations of love and the ways in which it enters into interests and activities of all kinds. The child's early attachment to his mother's breast and to her milk is the foundation of all love relations in life. But if we consider the mother's milk merely as a healthy and suitable food, we may conclude that it could easily be replaced by other equally suitable food. The mother's milk, however, which first stills the baby's pangs of hunger and is given to him by the breast which he comes to love more and more, acquires for him an emotional value which cannot be overrated. The breast and its product, which first gratify his self-preservative instinct as well as his sexual desires, come to stand in his mind for love, pleasure and security. The extent to which he is *psychologically* able to replace this first food by other foods is therefore a matter of supreme importance. The mother may succeed with greater or lesser difficulty in accustoming the child to other foods ; but, even so, the baby may not have given up his intense desire for his first food, may not have got over the grievances and hatred at having been deprived of it, nor have adapted himself in the real sense to this frustration—and if this be so, he may not be able to adapt himself truly to any other frustrations which follow in life.

If, by exploring the unconscious mind, we come to understand the strength and depth of this first attachment to the mother and to her food, and the intensity with which it persists in the unconscious mind of the grown-up person, we may wonder how it can come about that the child detaches himself more and more from his mother, and gradually achieves independence. Already in the small baby there is, it is true, a keen interest in things that go on around him, a growing curiosity, an enjoyment in getting to know new people and things, and pleasure in his various achievements, all of which seem to enable the child to find new objects of love and interest. But these facts do not altogether explain the child's ability to detach himself from his mother, since in his unconscious mind he is so closely tied to her. The very nature of this over-strong attachment, however, tends to drive him away from her because (frustrated greed and hatred being inevitable) it gives rise to the fear of losing this all-important person, and consequently to the fear of dependence upon her. There is thus in the unconscious mind a tendency to give her up, which is counteracted by the urgent desire to keep her for ever. These conflicting feelings, together with the emotional and intellectual growth of the child which enable him to find other objects of interest and pleasure, result in the capacity to transfer love, replacing the first loved person by other people and things. It is because the child experiences so much love in connection with his mother that he has so much to draw upon for his later attachments. This process of displacing love is of the greatest importance for the development of the personality and of human relationships; indeed, one may say, for the development of culture and civilization as a whole.

Along with the process of displacing love (and hate) from one's mother to other people and things, and thus distributing these emotions on to the wider world, goes another mode of dealing with early impulses. Sensual feelings which the child experiences in connection with his mother's breast develop into love towards her as a whole person; feelings of love are from their very beginning fused with sexual desires. Psycho-analysis has drawn attention to the fact that sexual feelings towards the parents, brothers and sisters not only exist but can be observed to a certain extent in young children; it is only by exploring the unconscious mind, however, that the strength and fundamental importance of these sexual feelings can be understood.

Sexual desires are, as we already know, closely linked up with aggressive impulses and phantasies, with guilt and the fear of the death of the loved people, all of which drive the child to lessen his attachments to his parents. There is also a tendency in the child to repress these sexual feelings, i.e. they become unconscious, and are, so to speak, buried in the depths of the mind. Sexual impulses also get disconnected from the first loved people, and thus the child acquires the capacity to love some people in a predominantly affectionate way.

The psychological processes just described—replacing one loved person by others, dissociating to a certain extent sexual from tender feelings, and repressing sexual impulses and desires—are an integral part of the child's capacity for establishing wider relationships. It is, however, essential for a successful all-round development that the repression of sexual feelings in connection with the first loved people should not be too strong,[1] and that the

[1] Sexual phantasies and desires remain active in the unconscious mind and are also expressed to a certain extent in the child's behaviour and in his play and other activities. If repression is too strong, if the phantasies

displacing of the child's feelings from the parents to other people should not be too complete. If enough love remains available for those nearest to the child, if his sexual desires in connection with them are not too deeply repressed, then in later life love and sexual desires can be revived and brought together again, and they then play a vital part in happy love relationships. In a really successfully developed personality some love for the parents remains, but love for other people and things will be added. This is not, however, a mere extension of love but, as I have stressed, a diffusion of emotions, which lessens the burden of the child's conflicts and guilt connected with the attachment to and dependence on the first people he loves.

By turning to other people his conflicts are not done away with, for he transfers them from the first and most important people in a less intense degree to these new objects of love (and hate) which partly stand for the old ones. Just because his feelings towards these new people are less intense, his drive to make reparation, which may be impeded if the feelings of guilt are over-strong, can now come more fully into play.

It is well known that a child's development is helped by his having brothers and sisters. His growing up with them allows him to detach himself more from his parents and to build up a new type of relationship with brothers and sisters. We know, however, that he not only loves them, but has

and desires remain too deeply buried and can find no expression, this may not only have the effect of inhibiting strongly the working of his imagination (and with this of activities of all kinds), but also of seriously impeding the individual's later sexual life.

strong feelings of rivalry, hate and jealousy towards them. For this reason, relationships to cousins, playmates and other children still further removed from the nearest family situation, allow divergences from the relationships to brothers and sisters — divergences which again are of great importance as a foundation for later social relationships.

Relationships in School Life

School life affords an opportunity for developing the experience already gained of relationship to people, and provides a field for new experiments on this line. Among a greater number of children the child may find one or two or several who respond better to his special make-up than his brothers and sisters did. These new friendships, among other satisfactions, give him an opportunity for revising and improving, as it were, the early relationships with his brothers and sisters, which may have been unsatisfactory. He may actually have been aggressive towards, let us say, a brother who was weaker or younger ; or it may have been mainly his unconscious sense of guilt because of hatred and jealousy which disturbed the relationship—a disturbance which may persist into grown-up life. This unsatisfactory state of affairs may have a profound effect later upon his emotional attitudes towards people in general. Some children are, as we know, incapable of making friends at school, and this is because they carry their early conflicts into a new environment. With others who can detach themselves sufficiently from their first emotional entanglements and can make friends with schoolmates, it is often found that the actual relation to brothers and sisters then improves. The new companionships prove to the child that he is able to love and is lovable, that love and goodness *exist*, and this is unconsciously felt also as a proof that he can repair harm which he has done to others in his imagination or in actual fact. Thus new friendships help in the solution of earlier emotional difficulties, without the person being aware either of the exact nature of those early troubles or of the way in which they are being solved. By all of these means the tendencies for making reparation find scope, the sense of guilt is lessened, and trust in oneself and in others is increased.

School life also gives opportunity for a greater separation of hate from love than was possible in the small family circle. At school, some children can be hated, or merely disliked, while others can be loved. In this way, both the repressed emotions of love and hate—repressed because of the conflict about hating a loved person—can find fuller expression in more or less socially accepted directions. Children ally themselves in various ways, and develop certain rules as to how far they can go in their expressions of hatred or dislike of others. Games and the team spirit associated with them are a regulating factor in these alliances and in the display of aggression.

Jealousy and rivalry for the teacher's love and appreciation, though they may be quite strong, are experienced in a setting different from that of home life. Teachers are, on the whole, further removed from the child's feelings, they bring less emotion into the situation than parents do, and they also divide their feelings among many children.

Relationships in Adolescence

As the child grows to adolescence, his tendency to hero-worship often finds expression in his relation to some teachers, while others may be disliked, hated or scorned. This is another instance of the process of separating hatred from love, a process which affords relief, both because the ' good ' person is spared and because there is satisfaction in hating someone who is thought to be worthy of it. The loved and hated father, the loved and hated mother, are, as I have already said, originally the objects of both admiration and of hatred and devaluation. But these mixed feelings, which are, as we know, too conflicting and burdensome for the young child's mind and therefore likely to be impeded or buried, find part expression in the child's relations with other people—for instance, nurses, aunts, uncles and various relatives. Later on, in adolescence, most children manifest a strong tendency to turn away from their parents ; and this is largely because sexual desires and conflicts connected with the parents are once more gaining in strength. The early feelings of rivalry and hatred against the father or the mother, as the case may be, are revived and experienced with full force, though their sexual motive remains unconscious. Young people tend to be very aggressive and unpleasant to their parents, and to other people who lend themselves to it, such as servants, a weak teacher, or disliked schoolmates. But when hatred reaches such strength, the necessity to preserve goodness and love within and without becomes all the more urgent. The aggressive youth is therefore driven to find people whom he can look up to and idealize. Admired teachers can serve this purpose ; and inner security is derived from the feelings of love, admiration and trust towards them, because, among other reasons, in the unconscious mind these feelings seem to confirm the existence of good parents and of a love relation to them, thus disproving the great hatred, anxiety and guilt which at this period of life have become so strong. There are, of course, children who can keep love and admiration for the parents themselves even while they are going through these difficulties, but they are not very common. I think that what I have said goes a little way to explain the peculiar position in the minds of people generally of idealized figures such as famous men and women, authors, athletes, adventurers, imaginary characters taken from literature—people towards whom is turned the love and admiration without which all things would take on the gloom of hate and lovelessness, a state that is felt to be dangerous to the self and to others.

Together with the idealization of certain people goes the hatred against others, who are painted in the darkest colours. This applies especially to imaginary people, i.e. certain types of villains in films and in literature ; or to real people somewhat removed from oneself, such as political leaders of the opposite party. It is safer to hate these people, who are either unreal or further removed, than to hate those nearer to one—safer for them and for oneself. This applies also to a certain extent to the hatred against some teachers or headmasters, for the general school discipline and the whole situation tends to make a greater barrier between pupil and teacher than often exists between son and father.

This division between love and hate towards

people not too close to oneself also serves the purpose of keeping loved people more secure, both actually and in one's mind. They are not only remote from one physically and thus inaccessible, but the division between the loving and hating attitude fosters the feeling that one can keep love unspoilt. The feeling of security that comes from being able to love is, in the unconscious mind, closely linked up with keeping loved people safe and undamaged. The unconscious belief seems to run : I am able to keep some loved people intact, then I have really not damaged any of my loved people and I keep them all for ever in my mind. In the last analysis the image of the loved parents is preserved in the unconscious mind as the most precious possession, for it guards its possessor against the pain of utter desolation.

The Development of Friendships

The child's early friendships change in character during adolescence. The strength of impulses and feelings, which is so characteristic of this stage of life, brings about very intense friendships between young people, mostly between members of the same sex. Unconscious homosexual tendencies and feelings underlie these relationships and very often lead to actual homosexual activities. Such relationships are partly an escape from the drive towards the other sex, which is often too unmanageable at this stage, for various internal and external reasons. To speak of internal ones and to take the case of the boy : his desires and phantasies are still very much connected with his mother and sisters, and the struggle of turning away from them and finding new love objects is at its very height. The impulses towards the other sex, with both boys and girls at this stage, are often felt to be fraught with so many dangers that the drive towards people of the same sex tends to become intensified. The love, admiration and adulation which can be put into these friendships are also, as I pointed out before, a safeguard against hatred, and for these various reasons young people cling all the more to such relationships. At this stage of development, the increased homosexual tendencies, whether conscious or unconscious, also play a great part in the adulation of teachers of the same sex. Friendships in adolescence, as we know, are very often unstable. A reason for this is to be found in the strength of the sexual feelings (unconscious or conscious) which enter into them and disturb them. The adolescent is not yet emancipated from the strong emotional ties of infancy and is still—more than he knows—swayed by them.

Friendships in Adult Life

In adult life, though unconscious homosexual tendencies play their part in friendships between people of the same sex, it is characteristic of friendship—as distinct from a homosexual love relationship[1]—that affectionate feelings can be partially dissociated from sexual ones, which recede into the background, and though remaining to a certain extent active in the unconscious mind, for practical purposes they disappear. This separation of sexual from affectionate feelings can apply also to

[1] The subject of homosexual love relations is a wide and very complicated one. To deal with it adequately would necessitate more space than I have at my disposal, and I restrict myself, therefore, to mentioning that much love can be put into these relationships.

friendships between men and women, but since the vast topic of friendship is only one part of my subject, I shall confine myself here to speaking of friendships between people of the same sex, and even then I shall make only a few general remarks.

Let us take as an instance a friendship between two women who are not too dependent upon each other. Protectiveness and helpfulness may still be needed, at times by the one, at other times by the other, as situations arise. This capacity to give and take emotionally is one essential for true friendship. Here, elements of early situations are expressed in adult ways. Protection, help and advice were first afforded to us by our mothers. If we grow up emotionally and become self-sufficient, we shall not be too dependent upon maternal support and comfort, but the wish to receive them when painful and difficult situations arise will remain until we die. In our relation to a friend we may at times receive and give some of a mother's care and love. A successful blending of a mother-attitude and a daughter-attitude seems to be one of the conditions for an emotionally rich feminine personality and for the capacity for friendship. (A fully developed feminine personality implies a capacity for good relations with men, as far as both affectionate and sexual feelings are concerned ; but in speaking of friendship between women I am referring to the sublimated homosexual tendencies and feelings.) We may have had an opportunity in our relations to sisters to experience and express both the motherly care and the daughter's response ; and then we can easily carry them further into adult friendships. But there may not have been a sister, or none with whom these feelings could be experienced, and in that case, if we come to develop a friendship with another woman, this will bring to realization, modified by adult needs, a strong and important wish of childhood.

We share interests and pleasures with a friend, but we may also be capable of enjoying her happiness and success even when we ourselves lack these. Feelings of envy and jealousy may recede into the background if our capacity to identify ourselves with her, and thus to share in her happiness, is strong enough.

The element of guilt and reparation is never missing in such an identification. Only if we have successfully dealt with our hatred and jealousy, dissatisfaction and grievance against our mother, and have succeeded in being happy in seeing her happy, in feeling that we have not injured her or that we can repair the injury done in phantasy, are we capable of true identification with another woman. Possessiveness and grievance, which lead to over-strong demands, are disturbing elements in friendship ; indeed, over-strong emotions altogether are likely to undermine it. Whenever this happens, one finds, on psycho-analytical investigation, that early situations of unsatisfied desires, of grievance, of greed or jealousy, have broken through, i.e. though current episodes may have started the trouble, an unresolved conflict from infancy plays an important part in the break-up of the friendship. A balanced emotional atmosphere, which does not at all exclude strength of feeling, is a basis for success in friendship. It is not so likely to succeed if we expect too much of it, i.e. expect the friend to make up for our early deprivations. Such undue demands are for the most part unconscious,

and therefore cannot be dealt with rationally. They
expose us necessarily to disappointment, pain and
resentment. If such excessive unconscious demands
lead to disturbances in our friendships, exact repetitions—however different the external circumstances
may be—of early situations have come about, when
in the first place intense greed and hatred disturbed
our love for our parents and left us with feelings of
dissatisfaction and loneliness. When the past does
not press so strongly upon the present situation, we
are more able both to make the right choice of
friends and to satisfy ourselves with what they have
to give.

Much of what I have said about friendship between
women—though there are also important differences
by reason of the difference between the man's and
the woman's psychology—applies to the development of friendship between men. The separation
of affectionate from sexual feelings, the sublimation
of homosexual tendencies and identification, are
also the foundation for male friendships. Although
elements and new gratifications corresponding to
adult personality enter—fresh—into a man's friendship with another man, he also is seeking partly for
a repetition of his relation to his father or brother,
or trying to find a new affinity which fulfils past
desires, or to improve on the unsatisfactory relations
to those who once stood nearest to him.

Wider Aspects of Love

The process by which we displace love from the
first people we cherish to other people is extended
from earliest childhood onwards to things. In this
way we develop interests and activities into which we
put some of the love that originally belonged to

people. In the baby's mind, one part of the body can stand for another part, and an object for parts of the body or for people. In this symbolical way, any round object may, in the child's unconscious mind, come to stand for his mother's breast. By a gradual process, anything that is felt to give out goodness and beauty, and that calls forth pleasure and satisfaction, in the physical or in the wider sense, can in the unconscious mind take the place of this ever-bountiful breast, and of the whole mother. Thus we speak of our own country as the ' motherland ' because in the unconscious mind our country may come to stand for our mother, and then it can be loved with feelings which borrow their nature from the relation to her.

To illustrate the way in which the first relationship enters into interests that seem very remote from it, let us take as an instance the explorers who set out for new discoveries, undergoing the greatest deprivations and encountering grave dangers and perhaps death in the attempt. Besides stimulating external circumstances, there are very many psychological elements that underlie the interest and the pursuit of exploring. Here I can mention only one or two specific unconscious factors. In his greed, the little boy has desires to attack his mother's body, which is felt as an extension of her good breast. He also has phantasies of robbing her of the contents of her body—among other things of babies, which are felt to be precious possessions—and in his jealousy he also attacks the babies. These aggressive phantasies of penetrating her body are soon linked up with his genital desires to have intercourse with her. In psycho-analytic work it has been found that phantasies of exploring the mother's body, which arise out of the child's aggressive sexual desires, greed, curiosity and love, contribute to the man's interest in exploring new countries.

In discussing the emotional development of the small child, I pointed out that his aggressive impulses give rise to strong feelings of guilt and to fear of the death of the loved person, all of which form part of feelings of love and reinforce and intensify them. In the explorer's unconscious mind, a new territory stands for a new mother, one that will replace the loss of the real mother. He is seeking the ' promised land '—the ' land flowing with milk and honey.' We have already seen that fear of the death of the most loved person leads to the child's turning away from her to some extent ; but at the same time it also drives him to re-create her and to find her again in whatever he undertakes. Here both the escape from her and the original attachment to her find full expression. The child's early aggression stimulated the drive to restore and to make good, to put back into his mother the good things he had robbed her of in phantasy, and these wishes to make good merge into the later drive to explore, for by finding new land the explorer gives something to the world at large and to a number of people in particular. In his pursuit the explorer actually gives expression to both aggression and the drive to reparation. We know that in discovering a new country aggression is made use of in the struggle with the elements, and in over-coming difficulties of all kinds. But sometimes aggression is shown more openly ; especially was this so in former times when ruthless cruelty against native populations was displayed by people who not only explored, but conquered and colonized.

Some of the early phantasied attacks against the imaginary babies in the mother's body, and actual hatred against new-born brothers and sisters, were here expressed in reality by the attitude towards the natives. The wished-for restoration, however, found full expression in repopulating the country with people of their own nationality. We can see that through the interest in exploring (whether or not aggression is openly shown) various impulses and emotions—aggression, feelings of guilt, love and the drive to reparation—can be transferred to another sphere, far away from the original person.

The drive to explore need not be expressed in an actual physical exploration of the world, but may extend to other fields, for instance, to any kind of scientific discovery. Early phantasies and desires to explore his mother's body enter into the satisfaction which the astronomer, for example, derives from his work. The desire to re-discover the mother of the early days, whom one has lost actually or in one's feelings, is also of the greatest importance in creative art and in the ways people enjoy and appreciate it.

To illustrate some of the processes I have just been discussing, I will take the well-known sonnet by Keats, ' On First Looking into Chapman's Homer.' [1]

[1] For convenience' sake I am quoting the whole poem, though it is so well known.

Much have I travell'd in the realms of gold,
   And many goodly states and kingdoms seen ;
   Round many western islands have I been
Which bards in fealty to Apollo hold.
Oft of one wide expanse had I been told
   That deep-brow'd Homer ruled as his demesne :
   Yet did I never breathe its pure serene
Till I heard Chapman speak out loud and bold :

Keats is speaking here from the point of view of one who enjoys a work of art. Poetry is compared to ' goodly states and kingdoms ' and ' realms of gold.' He himself, on reading Chapman's Homer, is first the astronomer who watches the skies when ' a new planet swims into his ken.' But then Keats becomes the explorer who discovers ' with a wild surmise ' a new land and sea. In Keats' perfect poem the world stands for art, and it is clear that to him scientific and artistic enjoyment and exploration are derived from the same source—from the love for the beautiful lands—the ' realms of gold.' The exploration of the unconscious mind (by the way, an unknown continent discovered by Freud) shows that, as I have pointed out before, the beautiful lands stand for the loved mother, and the longing with which these lands are approached is derived from our longings for her. Going back to the sonnet, one may suggest—without any detailed analysis of it—that the ' deep-browed Homer ' who rules over the land of poetry stands for the admired and powerful father, whose example the son (Keats) follows when he too enters the country of his desire (art, beauty, the world—ultimately his mother).

Similarly, the sculptor who puts life into his object of art, whether or not it represents a person, is unconsciously restoring and re-creating the early loved people, whom he has in phantasy destroyed.

> Then felt I like some watcher of the skies
>   When a new planet swims into his ken ;
> Or like stout Cortez, when with eagle eyes
>   He stared at the Pacific—and all his men
> Look'd at each other with a wild surmise—
>   Silent, upon a peak in Darien.

Sense of Guilt, Love and Creativeness

Feelings of guilt, which as I have endeavoured to show, are a fundamental incentive towards creativeness and work in general (even of the simplest kinds) may however, if they are too great, have the effect of inhibiting productive activities and interests. These complex connections have first become clear through the psycho-analysis of small children. In children, creative impulses which have hitherto been dormant awaken and express themselves in such activities as drawing, modelling, building and in speech, when by means of psycho-analysis fears of various kinds become lessened. These fears had brought about an increase of the destructive impulses, and therefore when fears are diminished, destructive impulses also are lessened. Along with these processes, feelings of guilt and the anxiety about the death of the loved person, with which the child's mind had been unable to cope because they were overwhelming, gradually diminish, become less intense and are then manageable. This has the effect of increasing the child's concern for other people, of stimulating pity and identification with them, and thus love altogether is increased. The wish to make reparation, so intimately bound up with the concern for the loved one and the anxiety about his death, can now be expressed in creative and constructive ways. In the psycho-analysis of adults, too, these processes and changes can be observed.

I have suggested that any source of joy, beauty and enrichment (whether inner or external) is, in the unconscious mind, felt to be the mother's loving and giving breast and the father's creative penis, which in phantasy possesses similar qualities—ultimately, the two kind and generous parents. The relation to nature which arouses such strong feelings of love, appreciation, admiration and devotion, has much in common with the relation to one's mother, as has long been recognized by poets. The manifold gifts of nature are equated with whatever we have received in the early days from our mother. But she has not always been satisfactory. We often felt her to be ungenerous and to be frustrating us ; this aspect of our feelings towards her is also revived in our relation to nature which often is unwilling to give.

The satisfaction of our self-preservative needs and the gratification of our desire for love are forever linked up with each other, because they are first derived from one and the same source. Security was first of all afforded to us by our mother, who not only stilled the pangs of hunger, but also satisfied our emotional needs and relieved anxiety. Security attained by satisfaction of our essential requirements is therefore linked up with emotional security, and both are all the more needed because they counteract the early fears of losing the loved mother. To be sure of our livelihood also implies, in the unconscious phantasy, not being deprived of love and not losing our mother altogether. The man who is out of work and who struggles to find some has in mind first of all his essential material needs. I am not underrating the actual sufferings and distress, direct and indirect, which result from poverty ; but the actual painful situation is made more poignant by the sorrow and despair springing from his earliest emotional situations, when he not only felt deprived of food because his mother did not satisfy his needs, but also felt he was losing both

her and her love and protection.[1] Being out of
work deprives him also of giving expression to his
constructive tendencies, one most important way of
dealing with his unconscious fears and sense of guilt—
i.e. of making reparation. Harshness of circumstances (though this may be partly due to an unsatisfactory social system, and thus give actual
ground for the person living in misery to blame other
people for it) has something in common with the
relentlessness of dreaded parents, in which children,
under stress of anxiety, believe. Conversely, help—
material or mental—afforded to poor or unemployed
people, in addition to its actual value, is unconsciously felt to prove the existence of loving parents.

To go back to the relation to nature. In some
parts of the world nature is cruel and destructive,
but nevertheless the inhabitants defy the dangers of
the elements, whether these be drought, floods,
cold, heat, earthquakes or plagues, rather than give
up their land. External circumstances, it is true,
play an important part, for these tenacious people

[1] In the psycho-analysis of children I frequently
discovered—of course in varying degrees—fears of being
turned out of the home as a punishment for unconscious aggression (wishing to turn others out) and for
actual harm which had been done. This anxiety sets in
very early and may prey very strongly on the child's
mind. A special case of it is the fear of being either a poor
orphan or a beggar, and having no home and no food.
Now these fears of being destitute, with the children
in whom I have observed them, were quite independent
of the parents' financial situation. In later life, fears
of this kind have the effect of increasing the actual
difficulties which arise from such things as loss of money
or having to give up a house, or loss of one's work ;
they add an element of poignancy and deepen despair.

may have no facilities for moving away from the place where they have grown up. This, however, does not seem to me to explain fully the phenomenon that so much hardship can sometimes be borne in order to keep to the native land. With people who are living under such hard conditions of nature, the struggle for a livelihood serves other (unconscious) purposes as well. Nature represents to him a grudging and exacting mother, whose gifts must be forcibly extolled from her, whereby early violent phantasies are repeated and acted out (though in a sublimated and socially adapted way); feeling unconsciously guilty for his aggressive impulses towards his mother, he expected (and still unconsciously expects now in his relation to nature) that she would be harsh with him. This feeling of guilt acts as an incentive to making reparation. The struggle with nature is therefore partly felt to be a struggle to *preserve nature*, because it expresses also the wish to make reparation to her (mother). People who strive with the severity of nature thus not only take care of themselves, but also serve nature herself. In not severing their connection with her they keep alive the image of the mother of the early days. They preserve themselves and her in phantasy by remaining close to her— actually by not leaving their country. In contrast with this, the explorer is seeking in phantasy a new mother in order to replace the real one from whom he feels estranged, or whom he is unconsciously afraid to lose.

The Relationship to Ourselves and to Others

I have dealt in this section with some aspects of the individual's love and relations towards other people. I cannot conclude, however, without attempting to throw some light upon the most complicated relationship of all, and that is the one we have to ourselves. But what are our selves ? Everything, good or bad, that we have gone through from our earliest days onwards : all that we have received from the external world and all that we have felt in our inner world, happy and unhappy experiences, relationships to people, activities, interests and thoughts of all kinds—that is to say, everything we have lived through—makes part of our selves and goes to build up our personalities. If some of our past relationships, with all the associated memories, with the wealth of feelings they called forth, could be suddenly wiped out of our lives, how impoverished and empty we should feel ! How much love, trust, gratification, comfort and gratitude, which we experienced and returned, would be lost ! Many of us would not even want to have missed some of our painful experiences, for they have also contributed to the enrichment of our personalities. I have referred many times in this paper to the important bearing our early relationships have on our later ones. Now I want to show that these earliest emotional situations fundamentally influence our relationships to *ourselves*. We keep enshrined in our minds our loved people ; we may feel in certain difficult situations that we are guided by them, and may find ourselves wondering how *they* would behave, and whether or not they would approve of our actions. From what I have already said, we may conclude that these people to whom we look up in this way ultimately stand for the admired and loved parents. We have seen, however, that it is by no means easy for the child to establish harmonious

relationships to them, and that early feelings of love
are seriously inhibited and disturbed by impulses
of hatred and by the unconscious sense of guilt to
which these give rise. It is true, the parents may
have been lacking in love or understanding, and
this would tend to increase difficulties all round.
Destructive impulses and phantasies, fears and
distrust, which are always to some extent active in
the small child even in the most favourable circumstances, are necessarily very much increased by
unfavourable conditions and unpleasant experiences.
Moreover—and this is also very important—if the
child is not afforded enough happiness in his early
life, his capacity for developing a hopeful attitude
as well as love and trust in people will be disturbed.
It does not follow from this, however, that the capacity
for love and happiness which develops in the child
is in direct proportion to the amount of love afforded
him. Indeed there are children who develop extremely harsh and stern parent-figures in their
unconscious minds—which disturb the relation to
the actual parents and to people in general—even
though the parents have been kind and loving to
them. On the other hand, the child's mental
difficulties are often not in direct proportion to the
unfavourable treatment he receives. If, for internal
reasons, which from the outset vary in different
individuals, there is little capacity to tolerate frustration, and if aggression, fears and feelings of guilt are
very strong, then the actual shortcomings of the
parents, and especially their motives for doing the
wrong thing, may become grossly exaggerated and
distorted in the child's mind, and his parents and
other people around him may be felt to be predominantly harsh and stern. For our own hatred,

fear and distrust tend to create in our unconscious minds frightening and exacting parent-figures. Now these processes are in varying degrees active in all of us, since we all have to struggle—in one way or another and more or less—with feelings of hatred and fears. Thus we see that the *quantities* of aggressive impulses, fears and feelings of guilt (which arise partly for internal reasons) have an important bearing upon the predominant mental attitude which we develop.

In contrast to those children who, in response to an unfavourable treatment, develop, in their unconscious minds, such harsh and stern parent-figures and whose whole mental attitude is so disastrously affected by this, there are many children who are much less adversely affected by the mistakes or lack of understanding of their parents. Children who—for internal reasons—are from the beginning more capable of bearing frustrations (whether avoidable or unavoidable), that is to say, can do so without being so dominated by their own impulses of hatred and suspicion—such children will be much more tolerant to mistakes their parents make in dealing with them. They can rely more upon their own friendly feelings, and are therefore more secure in themselves and less easily shaken by what comes to them from the outer world. No child's mind is free from fears and suspicions, but if the relation to our parents is built predominantly upon trust and love, we can establish them firmly in our minds as guiding and helpful figures, whioh are a source of comfort and harmony and the prototype for all friendly relationships in later life.

I tried to throw light on some of our adult relationships by saying that we behave towards certain people as our parents behaved towards us, when they were loving, or as we wanted them to behave, and that thus we reverse early situations. Or again, with some people, we have the attitude of a loving child towards his parents. Now this interchangeable child-parent relation which we manifest in our attitude to people is also *experienced within ourselves to these helpful, guiding figures whom we keep in our minds.* We unconsciously feel these people who form part of our inner world to be loving and protective parents towards us, and we return this love, we feel like parents towards them. These phantasy-relationships, based on real experiences and memories, form part of our continuous, active life of feeling and of imagination, and contribute to our happiness and mental strength. If, however, the parent-figures, which are maintained in our feelings and in our unconscious minds, are predominantly harsh, then we cannot be at peace with ourselves. It is well known that too harsh a conscience gives rise to worry and unhappiness. It is less well known, but proved by psycho-analytic findings, that the strain of such phantasies of internal warfare and the fears connected with it are at the bottom of what we recognize as a vindictive conscience. Incidentally these stresses and fears can be expressed in deep mental disturbances and lead to suicide.

I have used the rather odd phrase ' the relation to ourselves.' Now I should like to add that this is a relation of all that we cherish and love and to all that we hate in ourselves. I have tried to make clear that one part of ourselves that we cherish is the wealth we have accumulated through our relations to external people, for these relations and also the emotions that are bound up with them have become an inner possession. We hate in ourselves the harsh and stern figures who are also part of our inner world, and are to a large extent the result of our own aggression towards our parents. At the bottom our strongest hatred, however, is directed against the hatred within ourselves. We so much dread the hatred in ourselves that we are driven to employ one of our strongest measures of defence by putting it on to other people—to project it. But we also displace love into the outer world ; and we can do so genuinely only if we have established good relations with the friendly figures within our minds. Here is a benign circle, for in the first place we gain trust and love in relation to our parents, next we take them, with all this love and trust, as it were, into ourselves; and then we can give from this wealth of loving feelings to the outer world again. There is an analogous circle in regard to our hatred; for hatred, as we have seen, leads to our establishing frightening figures in our minds, and then we are apt to endow other people with unpleasant and malevolent qualities. Incidentally, such an attitude of mind has an actual effect in making other people unpleasant and suspicious towards us, while a friendly and trusting attitude on our part is apt to call forth trust and benevolence from others.

We know that some people, especially when growing old, get more and more bitter ; that others become milder, and more understanding and tolerant. It is well known also that such variations are due to a difference in attitude and character, and do not simply correspond to the adverse or favourable experiences which are met with in life.

From what I have said we may conclude that bitterness of feeling, be it towards people or towards fate—and this bitterness is usually felt in relation to both—is fundamentally established in childhood and may become strengthened or intensified in later life.

If love has not been smothered under resentment, grievances and hatred, but has been firmly established in the mind, trust in other people and belief in one's own goodness are like a rock which withstands the blows of circumstance. Then when unhappiness arises, the person whose development has followed lines such as these is capable of preserving in himself those good parents, whose love is an unfailing help in his unhappiness, and can find once more in the outer world people who, in his mind, stand for them. With the capacity for reversing situations in phantasy, and identifying himself with others, a capacity which is a great characteristic of the human mind, a man can distribute to others the help and love of which he himself is in need, and in this way can gain comfort and satisfaction for himself.

I started out by describing the emotional situation of the baby, in his relation to his mother, who is the original and paramount source of the goodness that he receives from the outer world. I went on to say that it is an extremely painful process for the baby to do without the supreme satisfaction of being fed by her. If, however, his greed and his resentment at being frustrated are not too great, he is able to detach himself gradually from her and at the same time to gain satisfaction from other sources. The new objects of pleasure are linked up in his unconscious mind with the first gratifications received from his mother, and that is why he can accept other enjoyments as substitutes for the original ones. This process could be described as retaining the primary goodness as well as replacing it, and the more successfully it is carried through, the less ground is left in the baby's mind for greed and hatred. But, as I have frequently stressed, the unconscious feelings of guilt which arise in connection with the phantasied destruction of a loved person play a fundamental part in these processes. We have seen that the baby's feelings of guilt and sorrow, arising from his phantasies of destroying his mother in his greed and hate, set going the drive to heal these imaginary injuries, and to make reparation to her. Now these emotions have an important bearing upon the baby's wish and capacity to accept substitutes for his mother. For feelings of guilt give rise to the fear of being dependent upon this loved person whom the child is afraid of losing, since as soon as aggression wells up he feels he is injuring her. This fear of dependence is an incentive to his detaching himself from her—to his turning to other people and things and thus enlarging the range of interests. Normally, the drive to make reparation can keep at bay the despair arising out of feelings of guilt, and then hope will prevail, in which case the baby's love and his desire to make reparation are unconsciously carried over to the new objects of love and interest. These, as we already know, are in the baby's unconscious mind linked up with the first loved person, whom he rediscovers or re-creates through his relation to new people and through constructive interests. Thus making reparation—which is such an essential part of the ability to love—widens in scope, and the child's capacity to accept love and, by various means, to take into himself goodness from the outer world steadily increases. This satisfactory balance between ' give ' and ' take ' is the primary condition for further happiness.

If in our earliest development we have been able to transfer our interest and love from our mother to other people and other sources of gratification, then, and only then, are we able in later life to derive enjoyment from other sources. This enables us to compensate for a failure or a disappointment in connection with one person by establishing a friendly relationship to others, and to accept substitutes for things we have been unable to obtain or to keep. If frustrated greed, resentment and hatred within us do not disturb the relation to the outer world, there are innumerable ways of taking in beauty, goodness and love from without. By doing this we continuously add to our happy memories and gradually build up a store of values by which we gain a security that cannot easily be shaken, and contentment which prevents bitterness of feeling. Moreover all these satisfactions have in addition to the pleasure they afford, the effect of diminishing frustrations (or rather the feeling of frustration) past and present, back to the earliest and fundamental ones. The more true satisfaction we experience, the less do we resent deprivations, and the less shall we be swayed by our greed and hatred. Then we are actually capable of accepting love and goodness from others and of giving love to others; and again receiving more in return. In other words, the essential capacity for ' give and take ' has been developed in us in a way that ensures our own contentment, and contributes to the pleasure, comfort or happiness of other people.

In conclusion, a good relation to ourselves is a condition for love, tolerance and wisdom towards others. This good relation to ourselves has, as I have endeavoured to show, developed in part from a friendly, loving and understanding attitude towards other people, namely, those who meant much to us in the past, and our relationship to whom has become part of our minds and personalities. If we have become able, deep in our unconscious minds, to clear our feelings to some extent towards our parents of grievances, and have forgiven them for the frustrations we had to bear, then we can be at peace with ourselves and are able to love others in the true sense of the word.